Prayer:
Heaven's Open Door

Nancy McDaniel

Published by Aglow International

Printed in the United States of America

Library of Congress Cataloging-in-Publication Data

ISBN 978-1-60920-076-3

Acknowledgements

I have been greatly impacted and influenced in this project by the lives and teachings of Jane Hansen Hoyt and Graham Cooke. Both of these great leaders have been instrumental in my understanding and application of how to live from heaven to earth as a lifestyle and provided exponential growth opportunities as I have processed all matters of living in the atmosphere of God's Kingdom. As I have been greatly influenced by their instruction and modeling of these Kingdom principles, I have been transformed by the renewing of my mind (Romans 12:2). I honor both of them for their seeds of knowledge and wisdom that have been sown into my life and into the Kingdom. Their influence is reflected in many of the thoughts presented in this book.

Special Thanks

I wish to give a special word of thanks to several people who have inspired, encouraged and helped me in this book project. Jane Campbell, thank you for your excellence and encouragement in the editing process. Pam Eichorn and Sherry Gilmore of Ajoyin Publishing, thank you for your buoyant encouragement in this journey and your demonstration of how to finish well. Rick Allen, your cover art expresses the concept beautifully. Kay Rogers, thank you for managing so many details along the way. And of course, Dave, we are partners in every project—thank you for your loving support.

This book is dedicated to the countless intercessors around the world who bring the atmosphere of heaven to earth every day through prayer.

Contents

1

Your Life in Prayer

Ilearned a lasting truth about a meaningful life in Christ when I was young. I ran across a quote from Albert J. Wollen, that every Christian can enjoy "constant, conscious communion with God." Wow! Constant, conscious communion—being aware of God's presence in my life moment by moment, worshiping Him and talking with Him all the time in a practical, thoughtful way.

Those three simple words—*constant, conscious communion*—have marked my life ever since with the awareness that everything about life in Jesus Christ is 24–7. I can enjoy being with God no matter what I am doing; and He is interested in being with me, too. Those three words have been a benchmark to remind me that all the things we do to nurture our lives spiritually—things like prayer, studying the Bible, worship, loving one another and stewardship—all these things are not just what we do but who we are.

You Are in Christ

1 Corinthians 1:30 says, "You are in Christ Jesus; who became to us wisdom from God, and righteousness and sanctification, and redemption." And Colossians 1:27 says, "God willed to

make known what are the riches of the glory of this mystery among the Gentiles: which is Christ in you, the hope of glory." You are in Christ Jesus, and Christ Jesus is in you, the hope of glory. Our lives in Christ are not something we do, a theological opinion we carry, or simply a worldview. Our lives in Christ are who we are.

This applies to our prayer lives as well. Prayer is our life in Christ. It is who we are. Prayer cannot be separated from who we are, as if it is just something we do. Prayer is in us, and we are constantly in prayer.

A few years ago a friend of mine was asked, "When do you pray? Do you pray in the morning? At nighttime? Several times throughout the day?" Her answer was immediate. She said, "My life is a prayer."

Her reply accords with 1 Thessalonians 5:17: "Pray without ceasing." It parallels 1 Corinthians 6:19: "Do you not know that your body is a temple of the Holy Spirit who is in you, whom you have from God, and that you are not your own?" And it reflects Jesus' words in Mark 11:17 that "My house [or temple] shall be called a house of prayer for all nations."

I believe that includes you, since you are a temple of the Holy Spirit. Your very life is Christ's own house of prayer.

Praying in the Secret Place

As a prayer leader, I have participated in many big prayer events and highly networked prayer strategies. These thrusts, when God gives the directive, are powerful. How exciting and effective it is when the Captain of the hosts lines up troops of prayer warriors and gives the charge for them to take some major territory for His Kingdom. Yet I have come to realize that, while on earth, Jesus was more interested that His disciples learn to pray in the secret place.

2

His teaching and example, especially in Matthew 6, are essential to our understanding of prayer:

> "But you, when you pray, go into your room, and when you have shut your door, pray to your Father who is in the secret place; and your Father who sees in secret will reward you openly."
>
> MATTHEW 6:6

The secret place is vital to effective, life-giving prayer. Jesus still calls us today to learn the joy and power of knowing Him in the secret place of prayer. From that place, we will find ourselves empowered when the Captain of the hosts gives the glorious command for us to take territory for His Kingdom. When He does, we will take more territory, pray with more accuracy and see more of our prayers answered in growing levels of overwhelming victory. We will also find joy in knowing God in a magnitude beyond imagination as we meet with Him intimately in interactive prayer and worship in the secret place.

Last year my husband and I felt a longing to set aside a spot in our home as a secret place of prayer. We realized that, with a little redesigning of a portion of the house, we could set aside a room for us to spend private time with the Lord. At first, as we set out to decorate this special room, we considered what we both wanted and would find comfortable. But as we began to actually shop for the furnishings, it was as though the Lord said, *This is My room. I'll pick the furnishings.* We had not realized how much He wanted a room in our home. We experienced a complete shift in how we viewed it. It was no longer our room for Him; it became His room for us.

When Jesus said that our Father is waiting for us in the secret place, He was doing more than giving a clever word picture. He was sharing a profound truth. Our Father really is waiting and longing to spend time with us.

You may think of your favorite recliner, the side of your bed or the kitchen table as your special place to meet with Him. Yet the secret place of prayer and devotion is more a posture of the heart than a physical location. Whether or not you have a special place where you meet with the Lord, you carry the secret place within you. How can this be? Because Christ is in you and you are in Christ. In Him you live in that intimate place always.

Which leads me to two important questions (if we can be completely honest): Is your life with God life-giving or life-draining? And are you living in that intimate place?

We will look in greater detail at the secret place in chapter 3. But I want to explore the first question in the very next chapter.

2

How to Experience Life-Giving Prayer

Have you ever had occasion to use a plumb line? A plumb line is a cord with a weight attached to one end that is used to determine if something—say, a strip of wallpaper—is straight. It can also be used to determine the depth of a body of water. I have a certain question that I ask myself regarding nearly every area of my life. I think of it as a "plumb line" question because it helps me maintain balance and alignment. It also helps me know whether I am swimming or drowning in the deeper waters of life.

Here is the question I ask myself about any given activity: Is this life-giving or life-draining?

Since I know you will agree that prayer is essential to a vital and growing relationship with God, we need to ask ourselves the "plumb line question": *Are my prayers life-giving or life-draining?*

Prayer becomes life-draining when it is stagnant. Without the ebb and flow of a growing, vigorous relationship with God, it digresses into a one-sided recitation of our needs. We find little joy or satisfaction in prayer that is just maintaining a discipline or following a static pattern. I have a hunch God does not enjoy it much either. And where there is no life, there is little relationship, and no power or purpose.

But prayer does not have to be life-draining; it can be life-giving. In any vibrant relationship, the participants enjoy meaningful communication that includes getting to know the other person—his or her thoughts, ways and habits, dreams, delights—in a growing, dynamic way. It includes listening to his or her words, heart, expression and actions. There can even be dynamic interaction without a word being spoken, just in being together.

That is exactly what prayer in the secret place is.

I have discovered five ways we can experience this kind of life-giving prayer—ways we will explore in this chapter.

1. Know God

How do we pursue a vigorous, dynamic relationship with God? First, by getting to know the Father.

In the secret place, we learn His character in a way we will learn it in no other place. We can learn *about* God, His character and His ways, by studying Him in His Word, the Bible. But through prayer in the secret place, we learn the character of God by coming to Him directly, intimately. We approach our Lord face to face, so that when we pray, we know who we are talking to and who is talking back to us. This is the first way we find a vibrant, life-giving prayer relationship with Him.

In the secret place of prayer, we are drawn toward God's magnificence, His greatness, His majesty, His holiness, His faithfulness, His grace, His mercy, His kindness, His goodness. The secret place with Him is where we learn His unbounded favor toward us and discover the fullness of His goodness and delight.

Most of us have boundaries that limit our expectations of God's favor toward us. These boundaries come from a variety of sources. We may harbor wrong beliefs or personal insecurities or fears. The bottom line: We just find it difficult to believe how good God wants to be toward us.

We can spend a lot of time focusing on ourselves and trying to analyze why we live under such limited expectations. This introspection may be interesting and helpful, to a degree. We may even experience some breakthroughs that bring a certain sense of liberty and growing victory. Focusing on ourselves, however, will not free us from the box of our own limited expectations. At best, it will help us enlarge our box!

So how do we break through our limited expectations? Getting to know our Father in the secret place. It is here that the limits to our expectations of Him begin to dissolve. As we get to know Him better, we realize that He wants to bless us even more than we desire His blessings. Imagine that! And we receive a deep, unbounded revelation of His character that, as we pray, actually expands our expectations.

Prayer becomes life-giving when knowing God is a priority. Realizing that His grace and favor toward us are both unmerited and unlimited brings an amazing vigor and satisfaction to prayer.

2. Listen to Jesus Pray

The second way to experience life-giving prayer is by listening to Jesus pray.

Jesus is really into prayer. He is the great Intercessor. Hebrews 7:25 tells us that He can "save to the uttermost those who come to God through Him, since He always lives to make intercession for them." Romans 8:34 says that He sits "at the right hand of God" and makes intercession for us. The Son of God, at the right hand of the Father, is listening to His heart at all times. He knows the desires of the Father's heart deeply and intimately, praying the Father's good favor toward us.

When we quiet ourselves with God in the secret place and listen to how Jesus is praying, we learn how to pray ourselves. We will find no greater prayer partner than Jesus as we come into agreement with Him. And as we agree with what Jesus is already praying for us or for others, we are guaranteed to have our prayers answered according to the will of the Father.

Recently I was praying for a particular nation. I had been following stories in the news about critical economic issues, frustrated people rioting and all kinds of turmoil in that nation; so I thought I had some good ideas of how to pray. Yet as I quieted my thoughts and meditated on the goodness of my Father, I began to sense that Jesus was praying already in a different way.

My thoughts shifted from the mayhem in that country to a ministry leader I knew there. As I pictured her in my mind, I saw that she had a horrible gash on her head. I became concerned that she may have been injured in some way and began to pray for her healing, particularly in the area of her head.

The next day I received word that this woman had experienced a sudden seizure episode and memory loss. Although she did not have a gash on her head, I believe the Lord used the picture He gave me to draw my attention to her brain—the area of her body that needed prayer.

How did I know what to pray? Because I listened in the secret place to what Jesus was already praying, and I agreed with His prayers.

3. Observe the Holy Spirit

The third way to experience a life-giving prayer relationship with God is by observing the Holy Spirit.

The third Person of the Trinity fascinates me. He is so active. The Holy Spirit is the ultimate multitasker. While He is busy glorifying the Son and doing the will of the Father, He has taken on the disciples of Jesus—us!—as His makeover projects, with the goal of bringing us to marvelous maturity. The Holy Spirit is developing in us a greater capacity for the Kingdom of God. At the same time, He is wooing those who do not yet know Jesus into their own personal God encounters. The Spirit is not daunted by all these tasks; in fact, He loves the challenge.

The Holy Spirit is not some ethereal presence, or an "It." He is a real friend who is our Teacher and Guide. He moves constantly on our behalf. He is power. He is fire. And He sounds like a mighty rushing wind. He is the member of the Godhead who sets things into motion.

The Holy Spirit moves according to the wisdom and ways of God. As we watch Him move, we see how to cooperate with God as He forms His goodness in us.

Our lives, regardless of appearance, are no compilation of random situations and coincidental circumstances. Everything that happens to us and around us is part of the strategy of the Holy Spirit to draw our own perceptions closer to how God perceives us. One day the Spirit may set up an obstacle course to challenge our weaknesses and prepare us to move higher in the Kingdom. Another day He may shut the door to something we thought was the "perfect" opportunity—because He has the real perfect opportunity somewhere else. Then He may turn around and heap unexpected blessings on us just because He wants us to know the favor of the Father in a deeper way.

In the secret place of prayer, we learn to see the moving of the Holy Spirit in our lives through these situations and many more.

When we observe the ways and wisdom of the Spirit, we are also enabled to cooperate with how He is moving on behalf of others as we pray. We pray in agreement with what He is doing instead of praying our own "good" ideas or opinions; and we will speak accurately from the wisdom of God into the lives of others.

Participating with God as He unfolds His plans in our lives is an exciting way to live. It is exhilarating to cooperate with Him than rather wonder blindly what He is doing. It is satisfying to partner with God as He works in the lives of others. And it is astounding to watch how He orchestrates world situations and critical issues as we pray and partner with Him.

Romans 8:26–28 says,

> Likewise the Spirit also helps in our weaknesses. For we do not know what we should pray for as we ought, but the Spirit Himself makes intercession for us with groanings which cannot be uttered. Now He who searches the hearts knows what the mind of the Spirit is, because He makes intercession for the saints according to the will of God. And we know that all things work together for good to those who love God, to those who are the called according to His purpose.

Often we focus on "all things work together for good" part. Then the struggle begins. While we proclaim that God is working things together for our good, our hearts may be battling fear, doubt and unbelief. As we pray for more faith to really believe in His goodness, we may seek our own plan to make things work.

Sometimes the battle is between our intelligence (what we

see and know based on our earthbound experience) and our faith (what we see and know based on our dynamic relationship with God). It is as though we are afraid that to embrace faith fully will somehow lessen our intelligence. But faith does not lessen our intelligence; it increases it. How? Faith adds a spiritual or heavenly dimension to what we already know with our minds. Faith breaks through the limits of our earthbound thinking and gives us glimpses of God's thoughts and ways.

Romans 8:28 starts, "And we know that . . ." *How* do we know that all things work together for our good? Because we have an idealist's view of life? Because we have become so spiritual that we no longer use our natural intelligence? No, it is neither of these. Rather, we know that all things work together for our good because we have accessed intelligent, faith-filled thought from a higher dimension—that all things will work out for good for those who love God and are called according to His purpose.

We can know this because we know God through prayer in the secret place—in the three ways we have just discussed. Because . . .

We know the Father

First, in our dynamic, life-giving prayer relationship with God, we intimately know the Father. We know, in particular, that He is the champion of goodness for us. Jeremiah 29:11 tells us that God wants only what is good for us—to give us "a future and a hope." If we really know the Father, rather than simply know about Him, we know that He will work out only good things for us. Based on that premise alone, we can know that all things will work out for our good because our Father will do nothing to our detriment. Our Father is good, and He is good toward us.

We have listened to Jesus

We also know that all things work out for our good because we have been listening to Jesus pray. Jesus loves us, and His prayers toward us are favorable. We know that the Father simply cannot deny His Son. When we agree with Jesus in prayer, we know that all things will work together for our good.

We have been watching the Holy Spirit

And third, we know that all things work out for our good because we have been watching how the Holy Spirit has been moving on our behalf. In our dynamic, vigorous relationship with God, we see how the Spirit is working. God is never stagnant. Even if, on the surface, things may appear to be motionless, yet in the secret place we see that the Holy Spirit is constantly in motion answering our prayer. Knowing God in the secret place and seeing how the Holy Spirit works gives us empowering confidence. "The people who know their God shall be strong, and carry out great exploits" (Daniel 11:32b).

Do you want to carry out great exploits for God? I do!

4. Converse with God

The fourth way to experience a life-giving prayer relationship with God is through conversation with Him in the secret place. After the profound discovery of knowing the Father, and the tender yet strengthening confidence of listening to Jesus pray, and the exhilarating success of partnership with the Holy Spirit, we find that prayer is more than presenting the needs of ourselves and others to God. Prayer is, rather, an amazing heavenly dialogue with each of the Persons of the Trinity. Our prayers affirm the revelation and action of the Holy Spirit. Our conversation agrees with the authoritative intercession of Jesus. And our words reflect the heart, character, will and delight of the Father.

This is the conversation Jesus described in John 14:13–14:

> "Whatever you ask in My name, that I will do, that the Father may be glorified in the Son. If you ask anything in My name, I will do it."

He is saying, "Ask in agreement with Me." Jesus will do whatever we ask when we agree with Him. It is essential, then, that we tune in to how Jesus is praying. Then our prayers will agree with His prayers, and we will have what we ask.

What does this look like in day-to-day living? Sometimes we are not sure how to pray for certain situations. We readily see the need but are not sure of the best solution. In such times we can pray in agreement with Jesus.

One time, for example, my husband, Dave, and I knew God was leading me into a career change that would give more time for ministry. Yet we needed the income my present job provided. Should we pray for a miraculous source of income so I could quit working? Or should we pray for different work opportunity that allowed a more flexible schedule? We knew God could provide for us in any number of ways, and we sensed that the Lord had a plan that would allow a more flexible work schedule. With that insight, then, we could pray effectively in agreement with Jesus: "Lord, lead us to a creative work opportunity that fits in with the plans You have for our lives at this time."

Within a matter of weeks, we launched a flexible business that provided for our needs for several years.

I need to add that while we pray in agreement with Jesus, adding the phrase *In My name* is not some kind of password or secret access code tacked onto our prayer that enables us to access the boundless resources of heaven. (We do have access to those boundless resources, which we will explore in chapter 8.) Nor are we asking Jesus to endorse our own wishes with His heavenly seal of approval. No, when we pray in the name of Jesus, we are saying, "I fully agree with what Jesus has already prayed." We are praying a prayer of agreement with Jesus.

If God leads you to declare to someone, "Be healed in the name of Jesus," you are not reciting some magic formula. Rather, you are saying, "I agree with Jesus for your healing. Be healed because this is Jesus' will for you and because He has already prayed this."

Jesus instructed His disciples,

> "Again I say to you that if two of you agree on earth concerning anything that they ask, it will be done for them by My Father in heaven. For where two or three are gathered together in My name, I am there in the midst of them."
>
> MATTHEW 18:19–20

Jesus is present in power whenever we agree with one another in prayer. But He was stating a more important point as well—that when we come together in prayer, we are to do so in His name, in agreement with Him. It is not our agreement with one another that guarantees the answers to our prayers; it is our agreement with Jesus that gets results. He is the lead intercessor in our prayer group.

5. Make a Proclamation

The fifth and final way to experience a life-giving prayer relationship with God is through making proclamation.

A proclamation is a public statement or announcement, a declaration or decree.

Making a proclamation comes only after we have engaged in an inner-circle prayer conversation with God. Through the life-giving relationship of knowing the Father, listening to Jesus and watching the Holy Spirit, we gain a good idea of what God is doing on the earth. Our part, then: to step forward in confidence and full agreement with God, in the name of Jesus, to make a bold proclamation—another form of prayer that "carves a path" in the spiritual atmosphere to release the intentions of God from heaven to earth.

Proclamation prayer is speaking confidently to announce God's intentions. You and I get to declare what He has already set into motion. Isn't that amazing? Hebrews 4:16 says, "Let us therefore come boldly to the throne of grace, that we may obtain mercy and find grace to find help in time of need." Once we have obtained God's mercy and taken hold of His grace to help us in time of need, it is time to make a proclamation. We announce on earth what God has already established in heaven.

The best-known story about David in the Old Testament exemplifies the power of proclamation prayer. When I read the story of David in 1 Samuel 17, I see a young man who knew how to make a proclamation.

When the young shepherd boy came to fight Goliath with a sling and a few stones—having declined the heavy armor of King Saul—he came with the experience of victories already behind him. The youngest of eight brothers, David had spent considerable time caring for his father's flock of sheep. He had killed both a lion and a bear to protect the flock. Pretty impressive! Yet David had even more valuable experience: time in the secret place with the Father. In those hours alone in the fields, he had praised and worshiped his God, so that even as a young man, he knew Him intimately.

David drew his confidence facing Goliath, then, not from physical prowess alone. He drew strength from who God was—for him and for all Israel. He knew this was God's battle and that God always wins.

No doubt David was great with a slingshot. But it was not his skill with a sling that killed Goliath that day. Just before David released the stone into the air, he released a proclamation into the atmosphere that won the victory:

> "I come to you in the name of the Lord of hosts, the God of the armies of Israel, whom you have defied. This day the Lord will deliver you into my hand . . . that all the earth may know that there is a God in Israel. . . . The battle *is* the Lord's, and He will give you into our hands."
>
> 1 SAMUEL 17:45–47

When the future king of Israel—still a youth who could not handle the weight of King Saul's armor—released that powerful proclamation, it carved a path in the atmosphere that went straight for Goliath's head. David's stone could not miss. It was flying on the thrust of proclamation.

The old saying, "It's not what you know; it's who you know," is one of the secrets to powerful, effective proclamation prayer. Proclamations that cut through earth's atmosphere to bring heaven to earth are birthed in the secret place where we know God intimately. Effective proclamation prayer is the result not of reciting powerful words but of knowing a powerful God.

Experiencing Life-Giving Prayer

These, then, are five ways that will help you experience a vital and growing relationship with God:

1. Know God
2. Listen to Jesus pray
3. Observe the Holy Spirit
4. Converse with God
5. Make a proclamation

Each of these practices will help ensure that your prayers in the secret place are both powerful and life-giving.

3

What We Find in the Secret Place

Have you ever hidden a key in a secret hiding place? You might have concealed a house key in the garden or under a rock or planter to let a friend or relative in. You are giving whoever knows about the secret hiding place full access to everything in your home. In a way, the key gives permission for that friend or relative to access everything that belongs to you.

In the same way, God has set aside some keys for you. Here are just two:

> "The key of the house of David I will lay on [the Messiah's] shoulder; so he shall open, and no one shall shut; and he shall shut, and no one shall open."
>
> ISAIAH 22:22

And Jesus says,

> "On this rock I will build My church, and the gates of Hades shall not prevail against it. And I will give you the keys of the kingdom of heaven, and

> whatever you bind on earth will be bound in heaven, and whatever you loose on earth will be loosed in heaven."
>
> MATTHEW 16:18–19

God freely gives us these keys, and many more, to enable us to obtain all that He has for us. These keys give us access to the authority and power He wants to operate through our lives. The keys unlock the treasures and resources of heaven. With them He gives us permission to access everything.

But we have to know where the keys are hidden. Good news! Jesus tells us these keys are found in the secret place with the Father. We have already identified that place of effective, life-giving prayer:

> "But you, when you pray, go into your room, and when you have shut your door, pray to your Father who is in the secret place; and your Father who sees in secret will reward you openly."
>
> MATTHEW 6:6

When Jesus says, "But you, when you pray . . . ," He is setting apart our prayer from any self-inflicted sense of piety. In these simple words He is saying, "You are unique. For you, prayer is not about religion. For you, prayer is about relationship."

Jesus' teaching on prayer is profound in its simplicity and absolutely essential to a life-giving lifestyle of prayer. And the place He describes as our prayer destination is a special place, a place set apart, a "secret place." When we go there, we can expect to find a wealth of resources. In this chapter we will look at some of them.

Life from the Father

Sometimes prayer is a reaction to an urgent situation. The Lord welcomes these prayers. But Jesus placed a special priority on intentional, regular prayer alone with the Father.

The secret place is unhindered by distraction and not weighed down by spiritual warfare. It is a hidden place alone with the Father. It is unaffected by all the things that drain us of life; we actually find life there by the Father's presence.

It sounds refreshing, peaceful and joyful, doesn't it?

Jesus also says that our Father is already there waiting for us. We do not have to evoke the "right" atmosphere or even invite Him. He sees us the moment we enter and is waiting to bless us and lavish us with His good favor.

Other types of prayer and prayer strategies are good and have great value. When it is time to go to the high places to make decrees and take spiritual territory, we will go. When we need a word of wisdom or prayer of faith in an emergency, we will pray eagerly. When it is time to gather a community of believers as a prayer force to establish something of God's Kingdom, we will rally to the call.

But we will find power in these modes of prayer only if we have first prayed as Jesus taught: "But you, when you pray, go into your room." From that room alone with the Father, we are empowered to pray all other prayers effectively.

The Treasures of God

Jesus said, "But you, when you pray, go into your room." In some translations *your room* is presented as "your closet" or "your most private place" or "your hidden chamber." This is where we get the idea of the prayer closet. But the phrase Jesus used could also be translated "God's treasure room."

The houses of Jesus' day were not equipped with elaborate locks or security systems. They had no surveillance cameras or alarms that would shriek to frighten away burglars. So to provide a special place for valuables, so thieves could not steal them while the owners were away, homes were often built with a hidden room. This is the word picture Jesus used of the place where He told His disciples to meet the Father in prayer.

When you go into that room, Jesus said, you will not be alone; your Father is already there waiting for you. It is His secret place, you see, His treasure room. It is where He keeps His valuables—all the resources of heaven and the good favor of His lovingkindness toward you. He holds the key to your healing in that room, and the key to the anointing you have desired. He keeps the key to creative business plans that the world has not yet seen, and the key to mend a broken heart— and so much more.

He is waiting there to lavish it on you in His secret place— His treasure room.

The Place of Open Reward

Jesus goes on to say, "Your Father who sees in secret will reward you openly."

The Father reveals the majesty of His character, glory, goodness and kindness to you in intimacy, in the hidden place with Him.

The Son of God helps to align your prayers with His by letting you hear Him pray in that secret place.

The Spirit of God teaches you, forms the purposes of God in you and guides you toward higher thoughts in knowing the ways of God in this place. He hears the longings of your heart, your dreams and your needs as you enter that heavenly conversation with Him.

While God sees in secret, He rewards you openly. *Openly* means publicly and tangibly, in a way you can touch and see. *Openly* implies a demonstration of the goodness of God that everyone around you can see, too. *Openly* means "to spring open suddenly." It suggests abundance. When it is time for God to answer your prayers, He throws open the door, shines a spotlight on His blessing and tunes up the band for some celebration music. He rewards you openly.

Often we know in our hearts that there has been a breakthrough when we have prayed earnestly about a situation. Things need to be established in the spiritual realm before we see them manifested in the physical realm. Yet it is hard to be satisfied with sensing a breakthrough when we have not seen our circumstances change one bit.

When the Father rewards us openly, however, He does not hold back. He does not expect us to be satisfied with simply sensing a breakthrough. He demonstrates His goodness visibly. He puts the answers to our prayers right there in our hands where we can see them. A short worship chorus I heard a number of years ago in Sweden expressed this. It said, loosely translated, "Jesus is putting into our hands what we have seen only with our hearts."

John 10:10 adds further importance to this rich picture of the secret place with God:

> "The thief does not come except to steal, and to kill, and to destroy. I have come that they may have life, and that they may have it more abundantly."

Jesus wants you to come to the secret place with Him where you are untouched by the wicked one, who has a life-draining strategy for each of us. The thief cannot hinder you in that secret place. The thief cannot steal the goodness of God or His favor toward you. Nor can the thief remove you from the loving care of God. He cannot move you from your position in Christ. In fact, he cannot even find you there. Why? Because it is the *secret* place where "your life is hidden with Christ in God" (Colossians 3:3).

And the reward? The treasury of God, His abundance given to you openly and freely. *Abundance* means "excessive, overflowing, surplus, more than enough, above the ordinary." Now that is breakthrough!—the open reward of life-giving prayer.

The abundance of God's treasury is more than enough to meet every need you have and to empower you for any situation you encounter. His treasury is provision to advance you toward full and fruitful Kingdom life. So Paul writes,

> For this reason I bow my knees to the Father of our Lord Jesus Christ, from whom the whole family in heaven and earth is named, that He would grant you, according to the riches of His glory, to be strengthened with might through His Spirit in the inner man, that Christ may dwell in your hearts through faith; that you, being rooted and grounded in love, may be able to comprehend with all the saints what is the width and length and depth and height— to know the love of Christ which passes knowledge; that you may be filled with all the fullness of God. Now to Him who is able to do exceedingly abundantly above all that we ask or think, according to the power that works in us, to Him be glory in the church by Christ Jesus to all generations, forever and ever. Amen.
>
> Ephesians 3:14–21

God wants to lavish His treasury on you. His goodness compels Him to give you even more than what you think would meet your needs. He gives you Himself.

A Stockpile of Benefits

We invest in God's treasury in the secret place through our worship and prayer. The Bible says that heaven stores our prayers in "golden bowls full of incense, which are the prayers of the saints" (Revelation 5:8) and that God collects our tears poured out in secret "in [His] bottle" (Psalm 56:8). The Bible also compares our prayer and worship to rain and snow:

> "For as the rain comes down, and the snow from heaven, and do not return there, but water the earth, and make it bring forth and bud, that it may give seed to the sower and bread to the eater, so shall My word be that goes forth from My mouth; it shall not return to Me void, but it shall accomplish what I please, and it shall prosper in the thing for which I sent it."
> ISAIAH 55:10–11

> "Have you entered the treasury of snow, or have you seen the treasury of hail, which I have reserved for the time of trouble, for the day of battle and war?"
> JOB 38:22–23

The ways that rain and snow accumulate give insight, from these two Scriptures, into how we invest prayer and worship in the treasury of heaven.

Rain and snow accumulate in the upper atmosphere of the earth, in the region of the clouds, before falling to earth.

Water condenses in layers around miniscule particulate matter in the air, such as dust or salt. As the water condenses around those pieces of matter, rain or snow or hail is formed in layer after layer. Eventually those layers become so heavy that they cannot be restrained and they fall to earth.

When the layers fall to the ground as snow, it may form a snowpack in a mountainous area as layers of snow accumulate. That snow usually melts during the warmer months. A snowpack is important as a water source to feed rivers and streams as it melts. A winter snowpack in the mountains will water the valley below in the heat of summer.

I live in a large agricultural valley in California, the San Joaquin Valley. This valley grows much of the produce for the United States, and it is even considered a breadbasket to the world. The part of the valley where I live is also very dry, right in the foothills west of the Sequoias. With farming as a main industry, water for irrigation is a constant concern. We watch the mountains in the east during the winter months to see how much snowpack accumulates. The more snowpack builds up in the winter, the greater the water supply in the heat of summer. With a full water supply in the summer, we will see an abundant harvest in the fall.

What does the cycle of rain and snow in the mountains have to do with prayer and worship? It illustrates how we invest in the treasury of the secret place through prayer and worship. God's treasury provides for both withdrawal and deposits. So far we have looked only at how God lavishes His treasures on us as He rewards us openly. Yet in Scripture we see that the time we invest in worship and prayer in the secret place is a deposit that, like snowpack, will release benefits when they are needed most.

How does it work?

Consider again how rain is formed in the clouds, and

compare that to how we offer ourselves in worship and prayer in the secret place. In 2 Corinthians 4:7 Paul calls us "earthen vessels." We bring what we have to offer—worship and prayer—into that heavenly conversation in the secret place. God breathes on our offering. The moisture of His breath accumulates, so to speak, until rain begins to form in the heavenlies. That rain grows in the weightiness of heaven as we continue to worship God. Then the season comes when God thunders from heaven and says, "It's time for a downpour!" And our response comes with a proclamation: "O God, let it rain!" His rain refreshes and revives us. It is life-giving and brings a harvest.

Or consider snow on the mountains. The snowpack is the worship and prayer we offer on the mountain of the Lord, the storehouse of prayer and worship as we celebrate through blessed times and weep through difficult times. Job refers to the treasury of snow and hail as reserve "for the day of battle and war" (verse 23). As the warmth of God's presence touches that snowpack, what has been held in reserve for the day of trouble melts into life-giving waters of salvation, deliverance and rivers of joy. This snowpack also releases spiritual harvest.

So when we feel dry and unproductive, this is not the time to work harder or pray harder. It is the time to warm up to the presence of God in the secret place. Living water will flood our fields to produce a bountiful harvest.

The Secrets of God's Wisdom

Did you know that God has secrets? Moses said,

> "The secret things belong to the Lord our God, but those things which are revealed belong to us and to

our children forever, that we may do all the words
of this law."

DEUTERONOMY 29:29

Where are His secrets found? Yes, in the secret place.

God's secrets bring revelation for timely situations. We
can talk with one another and seek wise counsel from godly
people. Yet if we want God's wisdom, we must go into the
secret place and seek wisdom directly from Him.

People often ask me to pray for them because they need
wisdom from God. I usually start by asking if they have
asked Him yet. While I am happy to pray with them, I am
always puzzled by those who have not already asked Him
for wisdom. I understand that we all need help sometimes in
hearing and understanding the Lord. Yet God is faithful to
reveal His wisdom and give direction when we ask Him. The
greatest, most timely revelation of His wisdom comes in the
secret place with Him.

Some secrets belong to Him

The passage from Deuteronomy says that "the secret things
belong to the Lord." Some things are simply not ours to understand. They are the Lord's secrets, and we will never have
the answers or inside track on them.

We may also occasionally have questions that seem to go
unanswered. God does not withhold information or answers
from us to exclude us, isolate us or reject us. He delights in
answering us and helping us understand His ways. He loves
a good question. Yet He also has some secrets that are His
and His alone.

In the life-giving prayer relationship in the secret place, we
know our Father well enough to trust Him with His secrets.
We know His lovingkindness and goodness to such a depth

that we do not feel afraid or rejected when He does not answer all our questions. We find the strength and courage to go on joyfully without knowing every answer. We have the comfort we need to trust Him ardently in the issues we may never understand.

Some secrets belong to us

Deuteronomy 29:29 goes on to say that revealed things "belong to us . . ." For all the secrets that belong to God alone, there is much more in the secret place that He wants to open up and reveal to us.

Moses said that the revealed things belong *to us*. When something belongs to us, it is ours. We possess it and hold onto it. We treasure it, value it and honor it. We pursue it and protect it. There is substance to the Lord's revelation that we can hold onto and treasure. Christ is our Rock, and the understanding we gain in the secret place is the anchor that holds us to that Rock.

Some secrets belong to our children

Moses also said that the revealed things "belong to us and to our children forever." This implies that some of what we gain in the secret place are aspects of our inheritance. God will reveal truths to us in the secret place that He intends for us to impart to our children—both our natural children and our spiritual children. This includes people within our realm of influence.

The phrase *and to our children* speaks to us of something else, too. Often when the Bible uses language that implies generations, He is speaking of our spiritual inheritance. The secret place is where we apprehend the revelation of our inheritance. It is where we grasp the dreams God has for us and how those dreams will give birth to ministries or business plans or creative expressions of God's favor toward us.

You have an inheritance in the Lord, and the secret place is where you must go to find it out. There are life-giving truths in God's Word that He wants to unlock to you. He wants to say to you, "This is your inheritance; I am giving it to you."

When you draw near to God, you realize who He is in you and who you are in Him. The knowledge that you are in Christ—"your life is hidden with Christ in God" (Colossians 3:3), as we saw earlier—becomes a vibrant, life-giving reality. His presence surrounds you always, and you find a depth of His life flowing in you.

One day I sensed the Lord speaking to me gently. He said that it was a day for me to ask Him for something special. This was a surprise favor from God. I knew it was a milestone moment and wanted to be sure I asked for the right thing. My first question was, *What shall I ask?* Then, as I began to journal His response, I sensed Him saying that I should ask for the fullness of my inheritance so I could pass it to my children; and He went on to expound on some of the deeper meaning.

I knew He was not talking about my natural children because I don't have any. (Some things don't need a special word from the Lord to figure out!) I realized how important it was for me to receive wisdom in the secret place. He had plans for me that included the release of wisdom and revelation that would affect others. Revelation and strategies in His Kingdom, which He intended for me to share with others, were my inheritance that He would unfold to me in the secret place.

So that we may obey God

Finally Moses said that the revealed things belong to us and to our children "that we may do all the words of this law." Revelation is more than just knowledge, you see, or something to contemplate, or even thoughts that challenge our own thinking. Revelation is the power to obey what God has said in His Word.

Deuteronomy 28, the chapter prior the verse we have been looking at, is one of blessing and cursing. It says, to sum it up, that if you obey God, you will be blessed with God's grace and favor in every area of your life; and that if you disobey God, you will be cursed living outside the favor of God.

The power of revelation, therefore, is critical. It can make the difference between a life of overwhelming blessing and a life of destruction.

The revelation we receive in the secret place provides the power to break the curse of disobedience off our lives. How? As we know the Lord and see how He is working in our lives, we step eagerly out of patterns of disobedience. Knowing Him in this life-giving way causes us to flee the unredeemed works of the flesh and embrace the life Christ has for us and the fruit of the Holy Spirit flowing through us. Revelation is the power to obey and receive His blessing.

Life Out of God's Fullness

Life in the secret place is full. God does not withhold Himself from us. We can access the treasury of God and live out of the fullness of who God is.

One of the principles Jesus taught in the parable of the wise and foolish virgins (Matthew 25) is the principle of living out of the fullness or abundance of the Spirit. The wise virgins had a plenteous supply of oil. They did not wait for an emergency to rush out to buy oil. They maintained a generous supply within their own lamps. The foolish virgins, on the other hand, let their lamps go empty. They waited until the last minute and expected others to provide oil for them. They tried to get by on empty.

This is a picture of a life-giving relationship in the secret place. We can choose, like the wise virgins, to live in a state of fullness, ready for anything at any time. Or we can be like the foolish virgins when crisis arises and go into a frenzy, looking for someone else to pray because we are just too empty to do so.

In computer science, the term *default setting* defines those preferences that are assigned automatically. Default settings remain in effect unless canceled, changed or overridden by the operator. In the same way, without a life-giving prayer relationship in the secret place, our default setting is like that of the foolish virgins: *empty*. We may go to church or Bible study to fill us up a bit and get us through a day or two. But we don't stay full for long. Soon life challenges us again and our oil gets used up.

A life-giving relationship in the secret place resets our default setting to *full*. When crisis comes, we are full of the anointing and presence of God, ready with powerful prayer and life-giving worship. And when we have a bad day or life gets tough and draining, we default back to full.

You will receive joy and life with God in the secret place. You will find reward and treasure with Him. And He is waiting for you there.

4

The Dilemma of Unanswered Prayer

God hears and answers our prayers. How do we know? Because God's Word says so:

"I say to you, ask, and it will be given to you; seek, and you will find; knock, and it will be opened to you. For everyone who asks receives, and he who seeks finds, and to him who knocks it will be opened."

LUKE 11:9–10

"Most assuredly, I say to you, he who believes in Me, the works that I do he will do also; and greater works than these he will do, because I go to My Father. And whatever you ask in My name, that I will do, that the Father may be glorified in the Son. If you ask anything in My name, I will do it."

JOHN 14:12–14

Now this is the confidence that we have in Him, that if we ask anything according to His will, He hears us. And if we know that He hears us, whatever we ask, we know that we have the petitions that we have asked of Him.

1 John 5:14–15

It is settled, then. God hears and answers prayer.

But what about *your* prayers? Do you feel they are effective, or are they sort of hit or miss? Do most of your prayers get answered, or are you settling for a barely passing grade? Do you keep praying and believing because you know God is faithful to His Word, or are you just hoping He might eventually do what you ask?

If it seems that your prayers are getting mediocre results, you are living below the abundant life God has for you. He wants you to live with joy, peace and confidence, knowing He is answering Your prayers fully, according to His Word. He wants to demonstrate His goodness to you and draw you into a deep relationship with Him as you pray.

A simple change in location will elevate the fulfillment of your prayers.

Where Are You Praying From?

We often hear the secret of real estate value and business success: "Location, location, location." It means that identical homes can be worth more or less (or that identical businesses might flourish or fail) based on where they are situated.

Location matters, too, with regard to prayer.

The dilemma of unanswered prayer has nothing to do with God's ability to hear or His desire to answer. Nor is it a deficiency in our faith. The Lord delights in doing good things and showing His kindness toward us. He wants to answer our prayers—not because of the greatness of our faith but because of the greatness of God Himself. It does not take great faith to get great results. A mustard seed portion, Jesus said, is enough to move a mountain (see Matthew 17:20). So the question is, Where are you praying from?

There are basically two prayer locations. I am not talking about physical location, but the posture of the heart. One of these locations is the "triage emergency room" and the other is the secret place.

Triage prayer

In terms of medical response, triage is the initial emergency care given on the battlefield or in a disaster where there are many victims. People are classified quickly according to their needs and probability of survival. They receive rudimentary care to sustain them until more detailed examinations and procedures can be provided. Many lives have been saved by quick and efficient triage methods.

Unfortunately, we have become conditioned to pray by the triage method. A need comes to our attention and we pray quickly with the handiest pleas and promises that come to mind. Prayer becomes a rush from one crisis to the next. It leaves us feeling flustered and anxious rather than calm and joyful.

Triage prayer has value. Like its medical equivalent, it can save lives. But it can also drain us of life.

As a prayer leader, I receive many requests for prayer. Many of these are for crisis situations. I used to think I needed to carry a burden of prayer for these emergencies. But I soon learned that no one can bear that weight or survive the frenzy of so many crises. Furthermore, I find nothing in Scripture that indicates we are to carry prayer needs in that way. 1 Thessalonians 5:17 says, "Pray without ceasing"; it does not say to run from crisis to crisis in a frenzied state of crying out to God.

The Holy Spirit began to teach me that I don't need to engage in the panic of the crisis. There is a better way.

Prayer in the secret place

We saw in chapter 1 that we are a temple of the Holy Spirit and Christ's own house of prayer. Our prayers should be formed in the habitation of the Lord's presence as we build His house of prayer in our hearts.

This, then, is the other location we can pray from—when we step out of the atmosphere of earth's crisis and into the atmosphere of heaven's provision. Prayer is more effective when we have formed a life of prayer in the secret place.

There we are not driven by the pressure of need but drawn into the peace of God's goodness and the joy of relationship with Him. We step out of earth's bondage and into heaven's liberty; out of earth's sickness and into heaven's healing; out of an atmosphere of worry and anxiety and into an atmosphere of peace.

In the secret place we nurture a life-giving relationship that sees from heaven's perspective. We know the character of our Father in every situation that arises. We are confident that our prayers are aligned with the prayers of Jesus, assuring us that we are praying in His name and in agreement with Him. We know the comfort of seeing the Holy Spirit work on our behalf in any crisis. Out of our meaningful, ongoing heavenly conversation with God, we can even make powerful, anointed proclamations aligned with God's will (as we saw in chapter 2), and we are guaranteed an answer.

Some years ago my husband, Dave, was teaching at a school where there seemed to be overwhelming spiritual darkness. At the time he was the only Christian working at the school, and there were just a few Christians among the students. Many adults on the campus who should have been role models for the students lived as an open display of sin and evil. Many students were influenced by this darkness.

Dave and I quoted every Scripture we could think of and prayed in every way we knew to see God's grace break through the darkness at the school. We prayer-walked the campus. We proclaimed righteousness and worshiped the majesty of God. We anointed the entrances to the school with oil. We even planted scraps of paper with Scripture declarations in the ground across the campus. Yet despite our earnest prayers, we saw little change. In fact, the situation seemed to get worse.

So we decided to gather the few Christian students we knew to pray for the school with us. We invited them to gather around the flagpole for prayer, as many students across the nation do on that particular day.

This prayer gathering did not look like the beginning of a spiritual transformation. Besides Dave and me, only four or five girls had come to pray, and they looked a little scared. Yet for me, it marked the beginning of a journey toward more effective prayer.

You see, before I went to the flagpole to pray, I had a conversation with God. I said, "Lord, we have prayed everything we know to pray for this school, and nothing has happened. This is the last thing we know to do. After this, we need You to show us how to pray." That was the question we should have asked from the beginning.

But even though I had finally asked the right question, I was still not fully listening for Jesus' prayer strategy for the school. It took a question from one of the girls who met us at the flagpole that day to get my attention. She asked, "If prayer for our school is so important, why have you only invited us to pray this one day? Should we pray every day or at least every week?"

Her question caused me to begin to listen for Jesus' prayer strategy. As I listened, I thought of this Scripture:

> "If My people who are called by My name will humble themselves, and pray and seek My face, and turn from their wicked ways, then I will hear from heaven, and will forgive their sin and heal their land."
>
> 2 CHRONICLES 7:14

The last two words, *their land*, seemed to arrest my attention. Suddenly I realized that God gives this special promise to those who pray for *their land*. Up to that time, I had been praying against the darkness at the school. Now Jesus was showing me *His* prayer for the school—that people would turn toward Him so He could forgive and heal the deep wounds of sin.

Furthermore, He showed me that these few students joining Dave and me at the flagpole carried His heart for the school in a way that I did not. They loved their school, and school was the center of most of their attention. In a way, that school was *their land*. I understood that Jesus' prayer strategy included these students praying regularly for their school—their land.

After that first day at the flagpole, we began to meet each week for prayer. The spiritual "location" of our prayer changed. We no longer prayed triage prayers frantically covering one dark deed after another. We stepped out of the atmosphere of crisis and into the atmosphere of God's provision. We began to pray as Jesus was praying—with great hope and peace, since we knew He cared deeply for each student and employee.

By the end of that school term, approximately eighty percent of the students had joined the Warriors, a Christian club on campus. Students turned to Jesus every week. The lives of many employees were changed, and those who did not change moved to other jobs, with new Christian teachers coming to take their places. The spiritual atmosphere of the school was completely transformed. The light of God's majesty replaced the darkness that had been present. To this day, the school is known for its good and peaceful atmosphere.

What Kinds of Prayers Are You Praying?

When you face problems you don't know how to handle, instead of dashing in prayer from one crisis to the next, linger in the secret place, embracing the calm and peace of God's presence. God transforms any crisis by His presence while you rest in Him. What strength and rest you find when you build your house of prayer in the secret place! Your prayers are far more effective, too.

More answers and less stress—that is life-giving prayer.

Crises come up suddenly—a car accident or a heart attack or an earthquake. In an emergency we don't have time to meditate on the majesty of God, listen to Jesus pray, watch the movement of the Holy Spirit and have lengthy conversations with the Godhead about how we ought to proceed in prayer about the situation.

But even when time is short, what kinds of prayers are you praying?

Reactionary prayer

Reactionary prayer is formed in the triage emergency room of prayer from our reactions to crises, traditions and emotions. Unfortunately, it may not be aligned with the good will of the Father or in tune with how the Holy Spirit is already at work. If such is the case, reactionary prayer probably is not too effective.

Intentional prayers

A crisis is the perfect opportunity for a powerful weapon: an immediate proclamation that brings the atmosphere of heaven to earth.

Prayer formed in the secret place, unlike reactionary prayer, is *intentional prayer*, fully aligned with heaven. This is not an entreaty launched randomly into heaven in hopes of hitting the mark. Prayer formed from our heavenly conversation in the secret place is spot on for heaven; it is guaranteed to hit the mark.

If you are abiding "in the secret place of the Most High" and "under the shadow of the Almighty" (Psalm 91:1), you are filled with everything you need in an emergency to make a powerful proclamation that will release the will and favor of God on earth.

I received a phone call for prayer from a very distraught mother. Her son had been arrested, and it appeared that he might face some time in prison. She thought the arrest charges where trumped up and wanted prayer that he would be released immediately from custody. He was young and very afraid.

My heart went out to her, and it would have been my reaction, in the emotion of the moment, to proclaim his liberty. Instead, the Lord spoke instantly to my heart that this young man was exactly where he needed to be to encounter the Lord in a life-changing way. I did not know if he was innocent or guilty; I just knew that the Holy Spirit had been working in his life. So I prayed that Holy Spirit would arrest him by the presence of God and that he would be transformed to step into his full spiritual inheritance.

That is exactly what happened. The young man spent a short time in prison. While there, he met the Lord and was transformed into a strong man of God who, to this day, is a champion for Jesus.

I am grateful that, because Christ is in me, I have the right prayer to pray at the right time.

Keeping filled up

Let's look again to the parable of the wise and foolish virgins in Matthew 25 for a vivid image of living in the fullness of Christ.

The wise virgins kept a full store of oil, symbolic of the Holy Spirit, just as we do when we nurture a life-giving prayer relationship with the Lord. At the midnight hour, when the bridegroom appeared, they had what they needed. All they needed to do was draw on the reserve of oil they already had on hand, and the darkness of the hour was dissipated in the glow from their lamps.

Likewise, in our own midnight crisis, we can enjoy the brightness of the presence of God inside—His life, wisdom, peace and power—resulting from our habitation in the secret place. In that light comes the power to pray in agreement with Jesus and in alignment with the Father's heart, according to all that the Holy Spirit is already doing on our behalf. In the light of God's presence, we find answers from heaven.

The foolish virgins of Matthew 25, by contrast, had enough oil only for the moment. The midnight hour found them depleted and panicked. In the same way, if we pray only from crisis to crisis, we will find ourselves running out of oil, grasping for the peace of God. We will feel empty and anxious, seeking an answer or looking for someone to pray for us and replenish our supply of oil.

But Christ is already in us as habitations of the Holy Spirit. As we abide in His constant presence and live with the internal fullness and brightness of who He is, we find joy and peace and rest, even in crisis. How can this be? Because although turmoil arises and situations around us change, the atmosphere of God's presence never changes, and in His presence we are safe, unshaken and at rest.

5

Praying as Jesus Prayed

In recent years I have found new joy in the worship experience of repeating the Lord's Prayer as part of corporate worship. Since understanding that this is Jesus' model of prayer for the secret place, I have found myself closeted away with the Lord whenever I begin to quote this prayer, even when surrounded by a community of believers. The intent of what Jesus was teaching somehow draws me into that secret place with the Father regardless of the setting. Then, instead of my heart only being warmed by the human tradition of worship along with a community of believers, I sense the undeniable power of the Father's presence flowing from that life-giving prayer relationship.

This model prayer is the most quoted prayer in the Christian faith, and it is frequently quoted in corporate prayer. In many Christian traditions, it is included as part of the worship liturgy. Although this beautiful prayer has become a beloved tradition for public or corporate worship, Jesus taught it to His disciples as a model for private prayer in the secret place.

It started with a question from one of Jesus' disciples:

> Now it came to pass, as He was praying in a certain
> place, when He ceased, that one of His disciples

said to Him, "Lord, teach us to pray, as John also taught his disciples."

LUKE 11:1

At times I have been puzzled by this disciple's request. Jesus' followers had at least an average background in prayer. Prayer was not a new concept to them. Although they were not scholars or religious men by vocation, they were part of the Jewish community and already had the models of prayer they had been taught from childhood. Prayer was part of their community and cultural life. More than likely, they had participated in prayer at the local synagogue and the worship traditions in their homes. They could quote the prayers that had brought hope and victory to their forefathers. These traditions had given them strength and comfort.

So the disciples already knew about prayer, and they already knew how to pray. Why did they ask, "Lord, teach us to pray"?

Something Different About Jesus' Prayers

The key in Luke 11:1 (above) was not the disciple's question. It was not the words Jesus used in His prayers, nor His eloquent speech. The disciples had noticed something different about Him after He had been praying "in a certain place." What place was this? Not some physical location. Rather, Jesus had been to the secret place to pray. He prayed as though He actually knew the Father. He was infused with life, power and authority. And His prayers always got results.

The disciples had walked with Jesus and observed His incredible capacity for ministry—His spiritual virtue, His physical stamina, His internal calm. They saw that Jesus gained a deep inner strength and peace when He went to that certain place of prayer with His Father. When the crowds were pressing against them, Jesus was calm. He had power to heal regardless of how many people needed healing. If people were hungry, Jesus had miracles in reserve to provide food for them. He was always prepared with the right story to teach a profound principle. He responded with astonishing wisdom to the adversarial questions of the scholars and religious leaders. He always had a kind word for the discouraged, even a delight-filled embrace for the clamoring children.

So the disciples wanted what Jesus had; they longed to participate in the kind of prayer they saw in Jesus' life that brought relationship, power and results. They wanted to know how to pray the way He prayed.

The Power Behind the Model

In response to their question, Jesus taught His disciples this model prayer in the context of His teaching on the secret place:

> "When you pray, you shall not be like the hypocrites. For they love to pray standing in the synagogues and on the corners of the streets, that they may be seen by men. Assuredly, I say to you, they have their reward. But you, when you pray, go into your room, and when you have shut your door, pray to your Father who is in the secret place; and your Father who sees in secret will reward you openly. And when you pray, do not use vain repetitions as the heathen do. For they think that they will be heard for their many words. Therefore do not be like them. For your Father knows the things you have need of before you ask Him."
>
> MATTHEW 6:5–8

The following is the foundation of Jesus' teaching on prayer and a powerful model of how He prayed:

> "In this manner, therefore, pray: Our Father in heaven, hallowed be Your name. Your kingdom come. Your will be done on earth as it is in heaven. Give us this day our daily bread. And forgive us our debts, as we forgive our debtors. And do not lead us into temptation, but deliver us from the evil one. For Yours is the kingdom and the power and the glory forever. Amen."
>
> VERSES 9–13

While the Lord's Prayer is eloquent, its power does not lie in its eloquence. Although this model prayer covers many of the needs of the human condition, its power does not rest in the scope of topics it addresses. The power of this prayer is the *location* of the prayer: the secret place. Every aspect of this prayer is empowered by our meeting with the Father in a life-giving prayer relationship.

Jesus could address *Our Father* because of the intimate relationship of the secret place that brought a depth of revelation of the holiness of God in heaven.

He could pray with authority and power—"Your kingdom come. Your will be done on earth as it is in heaven"—because He lived from heaven to earth. He drew His strength from heaven to live with a Kingdom mindset on earth. He lived out of that heavenly conversation with the Father.

Jesus could trust God fully for His daily provision because He knew the character of His Father. He did not base His trust on a list of clever quotes or positive thoughts; He actually knew the Lord. His Father was goodness and kindness all wrapped up in love.

Jesus understood His Father's favor and mercy for forgiveness. Jesus Himself found the grace to forgive in that secret place alone with His Father.

Jesus knew how to overcome evil and He knew about victory over temptation. Some think that Jesus stood sinless in the face of temptation because He was God. No, He came to live on this earth in the flesh and faced temptation just as you and I do. He won every battle against temptation because He lived out of the fullness of relationship with His Father in the secret place. And Jesus taught His disciples how to go to the power source when they prayed.

The lesson for you and me: Go to the Father in the secret place for life-giving relationship.

Spending Time in the Secret Place

The secret place, as I have said, is a spiritual location and posture of the heart. It is not a quick visit with God or a touch of His presence. It is a constant, dynamic flow of relationship with God. It is a place of habitation with Him.

Although our life of prayer and communing with God is continuous throughout each day, our time alone with Him in quietness feeds this relationship. As we spend intentional time alone with God, we find our moment-by-moment habitation with Him filling us with life, strength and joy.

How do we nurture our relationship with our Father in the secret place of prayer?

Be still.

In Matthew 6:5–8 Jesus told us what not to do. He said we do not need to be loud or showy in the secret place: "You shall not be like the hypocrites" (verse 5). We have no need to try to impress God or get His attention. He is not drawn to our eloquence. He is not impressed by the length of our prayers. In fact, Jesus said we should not use a lot of words, especially repetitious ones. When He said, "Do not use vain repetitions as the heathen do" (verse 7), I believe He meant that we should not launch immediately into proclamations or an endless list of random requests.

God is actually attracted to our quietness, our stillness before Him. Although He delights in our celebration and appreciates our service, He is attracted to our stillness. That is why Jesus complimented Mary and chided Martha. He appreciated Martha's service, yet was drawn to Mary's stillness.

He reveals Himself to us in our times of stillness.

So, worship Him. Meditate on Him. Think deeply on the goodness of God. Ponder His boundless creativity and unlimited resources. And listen. Listen to Him speak. Listen to Him breathe—the breath of His Spirit. Listen to Jesus pray. Soak in the goodness, strength and wisdom of your Father.

"Be still, and know that I am God" (Psalm 46:10). If we really want to know God intimately, personally, we will know Him in stillness.

Lamentations 3:24–26: "'The Lord is my portion,' says my soul, 'therefore I hope in Him!' The Lord is good to those who wait for Him, to the soul who seeks Him. It is good that one should hope and wait quietly for the salvation of the Lord." So we rest in the goodness of God as we quiet ourselves in His presence. In that calmness, we see His provision and understand how to access the resources He has for us.

Job 37:14: "Listen to this, O Job; stand still and consider [meditate on] the wondrous works of God." We will hear the Lord in stillness as we meditate on His great ways and the demonstrations of His majesty.

Exodus 14:13: "Stand still, and see the salvation of the Lord." Quiet yourself and see the movement of the Holy Spirit.

Remember, observing the Holy Spirit is one of the ways we relate to God in prayer. We can see Him clearly in stillness as He works His intentions for our good.

Worship God.

Worship God in the secret place, in the still place. Worship Him from a deep place in your spirit, not with your mind or emotions overly engaged. Just let your spirit worship the magnificence and majesty of God. Let your spirit be overwhelmed with His greatness and deep lovingkindness toward you.

Listen.

I know my husband, Dave, so well that I can recognize the unique pattern of his breathing when I am close enough to him. In the same way, listen in the secret place. Press your ear close to the Father and listen to His heart. Listen to the prayers of Jesus, the great Intercessor. Listen to the Holy Spirit as He discloses rich truth and shows you His ways. Listen as He speaks through His Word.

Sometimes I like to listen to God breathe in the stillness. Get close enough to Him to recognize His breathing. There is strength, anointing, power and comfort in the breath of God. That is intimacy.

Pray what is on His heart.

Jesus said, "Your Father knows the things you have need of before you ask Him" (verse 8). When we present a list of needs, He already knows the list. Rather than asking for things quickly, then, what if we inquired of His ways? What if we asked, "What do You want, Lord?" What if, instead of asking Him to fulfill our dreams, we asked the Lord to share His dreams?

As you enter a heavenly conversation with God, first pray

what is on His heart. Continue in the flow of what you hear as you worship and listen to Him. You may find that some of your prayer requests are no longer relevant in light of what you have heard from Him. Some petitions may turn to thanksgiving as you realize how the Holy Spirit is already at work on your behalf. Or you may have found peace and comfort in the issues that had before seemed troubling to you.

Pray what is on your heart.

After you have talked with the Lord about the things that are on His heart, continue with the things that remain on your heart. Be sure to give Him time to speak into those things and to give revelation for the situations.

And worship Him.

Continue to worship God, offering thanksgiving for the wisdom and revelation He has given. Fully embrace the courage and peace He imparts. Celebrate His goodness in the prayers He is answering. More breakthroughs for the answers to our prayers are released during worship than during times of petition. So once you have asked Him for something, worship Him. He really is working all things for your good.

John 17:22 says, "The glory which You gave Me I have given them, that they may be one just as We are one." Jesus was one with His Father, and He earnestly desired that we also would be one with Him and with one another. If we love the Father as Jesus did, becoming one with the Father, we will see His glory and experience His power. We will know Him in that life-giving prayer relationship. We will pray as Jesus prayed—with power, with authority and with results.

Over the next few chapters, let's look at key phrases of this amazing model prayer.

6

Our Father in Heaven

"In this manner, therefore, pray: Our Father in heaven, hallowed be Your name."

MATTHEW 6:9

I have been blessed with a wonderful father, a dad who loves me and who seems genuinely to enjoy being with me. As I was growing up, my dad laughed at what I thought was funny, took interest in what I was doing and delighted in sharing his interests with me. We took long walks together and invented games. He helped me write my first term paper. He was quick to teach me and quick to stick up for me. It is easy for me, then, to find comfort, strength and intimacy in the words *Our Father.*

Others were not so blessed and find it harder to relate to God as Father. But approaching God in prayer as "our Father," regardless of the kind of father we grew up with, comes through knowing our Creator in the secret place. We call Him *Father* because of the intimate, life-giving relationship we have with Him through prayer. He is interested in us and delights to share His interests with us. He walks with us and helps us with our life projects. He teaches us and sticks up for us. We know Him intimately. He is our Father.

We can approach God in prayer as "our Father," too, because we have shared experiences with Him. That is foundational to our confidence in Him. Even today, I know that if I ask my dad for something, he will do everything within his resources and abilities to comply. Why? Because he is my dad, and we have enough shared experience for me to know that he loves me so much he just cannot deny me.

Jesus knew that about fathers when He said,

> "So I say to you, ask, and it will be given to you; seek, and you will find; knock, and it will be opened to you. For everyone who asks receives, and he who seeks finds, and to him who knocks it will be opened. If a son asks for bread from any father among you, will he give him a stone? Or if he asks for a fish, will he give him a serpent instead of a fish? Or if he asks for an egg, will he offer him a scorpion? If you then, being evil, know how to give good gifts to your children, how much more will your heavenly Father give the Holy Spirit to those who ask Him!"
>
> LUKE 11:9–13

Our Father delights in giving to His children. He delights in boasting about His children. He really thinks we are terrific!—and He wants the rest of creation to see how terrific we are, too. I especially like the way *The Message* translates a passage that brings out this point:

> So, my very dear friends, don't get thrown off course. Every desirable and beneficial gift comes out of heaven. The gifts are rivers of light cascading down from the Father of Light. There is nothing

deceitful in God, nothing two-faced, nothing fickle. He brought us to life using the true Word, showing us off as the crown of all his creatures.

JAMES 1:16–18

So when you start to pray, "Our Father," pause over that expression of intimacy and endearment. Let the experiences you have shared with your Father bring confidence that He delights in you and wants to give to you. Let the intimacy of the life-giving relationship you have with Him wash over you with strength, comfort and deep joy.

Prayer or Worry?

Shortly after giving His disciples the model prayer in Matthew 6, Jesus said three times (verses 25, 31, 34) that we should not worry. He said we should not worry about life—what we eat, drink or wear. Nor should we worry about the future. Instead, we should seek the Kingdom of God and live a righteous life. Then our Father will give us everything we need.

It is important to understand the difference between worry and a call to prayer. A concern for a particular need may come to your mind. Is that concern rooted in worry or is it an urge to pray? If you bring it into your heavenly conversation in the secret place and find life-giving hope and revelation, then it is a call to prayer that will result in God's intervention. If you find yourself overwhelmed and preoccupied, however, so that your prayer times are rehearsals amplifying the severity of the situation, then you are caught up in worry that brings anxiety, fear and frustration.

Ruminating over worry is not intercession. The Holy Spirit wants to bring you into a better, life-giving relationship. He is able to bring little comfort when you rehearse your worries before the Father. Instead, He wants to draw you out of anxiety and woo you into the internal peace of the secret place with your Father.

But some well-meaning people confuse a genuine call to prayer with worry. They seem to believe that dread over dismal situations is a mark of intercession. They look depressed and are depressing to be around. They are weary and often struggle with burnout.

Prayer should not be depressing. Intercession is one of the most joy-filled ministries in the community of believers. Why? Because in prayer, we worship the majesty of God and live in awe of Him. The Holy Spirit shows us how He is moving in impossible situations to bring people to amazing outcomes. We get a front row seat to watch the miracles of God.

Worry means "to divide into parts" and suggests distraction or preoccupation with situations or relationships that cause anxiety, stress and pressure. It means to be double-minded—having part of your mind on heavenly things and part attached to earth. It is as though part of you is seeking first the Kingdom of God, as Jesus said, while the other part is distracted with worry and anxiety.

Jesus said three times in Matthew 6 that we should not worry. We should not be double-minded. Our Father already knows about all the things we need for life (see Matthew 6:8 and 6:32). When we start to pray, "Our Father," our minds find the simplicity of trusting Him as the One who loves us, provides for us and has mapped out the future for our good. When our attention is focused on heaven, we stop worrying about the things on earth.

And when we pray, "Our Father in heaven," we are addressing God in His dwelling place. We are drawn into that secret place, His treasury, where we can have a heavenly conversation. Our perspective shifts from the worries of earth to the promises and possibilities of heaven. Our attention is lifted to the limitless resources and goodness of our Father rather than being confined to earth's concerns. We become single-minded on Kingdom thoughts rather than double-minded with worry.

So when you are unsure whether a particular concern is worry or a call to prayer, ask yourself the plumb line question: Is this life-giving or life-draining? If it is life-draining, you have probably slipped into worry. If your urge to pray brings hope and life, it is a call to the secret place of prayer.

"Holy Is Your Name"

The central facet of God's character worshiped in heaven is His holiness. With our own attention cast heavenward as we pray, "Our Father in heaven," we, too, catch a vision of God's holiness.

This is what happened to the prophet Isaiah. When the king died, Isaiah began to seek God for wisdom for the next step for the nation. As he prayed, he had a vision of worship in heaven. In that vision he saw angels surrounding the throne of God crying out in worship, "Holy, holy, holy is the Lord of hosts; the whole earth is full of His glory!" (Isaiah 6:3). The angels were in a continuous antiphonal song of worship. One group would shout and sing from one side of the throne, "Holy, holy, holy!" Another group would answer from the other side, "Holy, holy, holy!" This continued and multiplied as heaven was filled with the glorious echo of worship.

In that place of sublime worship, Isaiah entered what I call a "heavenly conversation" with God. The Lord showed him some of the things that were soon to occur, and Isaiah's own participation in His plan.

In this vision Isaiah experienced some intense worship; yet

it was no more intense than the worship we experience when we enter the secret place of life-giving prayer as we worship His holiness.

When we pray, "Holy is Your name," we recognize who God is and speak into His identity. This is a powerful aspect of prayer.

Peter did the same thing in his conversation with Jesus in Matthew 16:13–19. When Jesus asked His disciples how people saw Him, Peter's answer spoke directly into Jesus' identity: "You are the Christ," he said, "the Son of the living God!" (verse 16). In that moment Peter entered a heavenly conversation. How do we know? Because Jesus said that Peter had not made up that answer or gotten it from someone else. His answer came by revelation straight from Jesus' Father in heaven.

How did Jesus respond when Peter spoke into His identity? He responded with revelation that spoke into the identity of Peter himself, releasing him into his destiny—just as happened with the prophet Isaiah.

How does this relate to you? When you pray, "Holy is Your name," you speak into the identity of your Father. Then He speaks into your identity as well. He responds to you according to the way you are seen in heaven. He calls you by name and empowers you to live in the identity He has purposed for you. He discharges the very anointing and provision of heaven into your life.

So when you go into the secret place with your Lord, relate to Him as your Father and receive His love for you as His child. Then speak directly into His identity as a holy God. In the heavenly conversation that follows, you will find empowerment and anointing to live in your true identity as He sees you.

7

Praying from Heaven to Earth

"Your kingdom come."

MATTHEW 6:10

In the secret place, we pray with an acute awareness of God's design and involvement in the details of our own lives, as well as in the events and issues of world affairs. "Your kingdom come" is actually a relevant and radical prayer. We are praying proactively for the reality of God's Kingdom to invade earth *now*. Our prayers align with heaven to release a life-giving force from heaven to earth. This life-giving force makes a righteous impact on the systems of the world. We are creating an opening in the spiritual atmosphere of earth for God's ways, intentions, creativity and goodness toward man's thoughts, institutions, organizations and governing structures to be discharged.

When we consider the idea of praying God's Kingdom to earth, it is important to understand the two kinds of authority we as believers exercise: external and internal.

Praying with External Authority

First, we pray with the *external* authority of God's Kingdom, bringing the Kingdom into the atmosphere of earth. Jesus conferred this authority on His disciples (both then and now) when He commissioned them to do the ministry of the Kingdom in the earth:

> Then He called His twelve disciples together and gave them power and authority over all demons, and to cure diseases. He sent them to preach the kingdom of God and to heal the sick.
>
> LUKE 9:1–2

> Jesus came and spoke to them, saying, "All authority has been given to Me in heaven and on earth. Go therefore and make disciples of all the nations, baptizing them in the name of the Father and of the Son and of the Holy Spirit."
>
> MATTHEW 28:18–19

This external authority enabled Jesus' disciples to fulfill, to an exponential degree, the work of the ministry He started when He was here.

External authority is also the mantle God confers on believers when He places us in positions of influence to bring the atmosphere of heaven to earth. For example, He gives vision and wisdom to lead people to those He puts in ministry leadership positions. He gives a caring heart and the ability to mentor and guide people through every season of life to those He calls to pastoral ministry. He gifts worship leaders with sensitivity to the flow of the Holy Spirit in worship and the inspiration to draw others into God's Presence. When He calls and positions us in specific ministry roles, He places His authority on us to serve in these ministries. In the same way, when God calls us to a realm of influence in the marketplace, government or some other organizational structure, He sets His authority on us to bring His Kingdom purposes to earth.

Praying with Internal Authority

God also imparts an *internal* authority to us in the secret place of prayer. Jesus told His disciples that "the kingdom of God is within you" (Luke 17:21). Internal authority is the unwavering confidence that God will take care of us no matter what. It is the assurance that we can rest in His lovingkindness and favor. It is the quiet, internal strength we carry because of God's unshakable Kingdom (see Hebrews 12:28) within us.

So when we pray, "Your kingdom come," we are seeking the Kingdom of God with full confidence that God will take care of all our needs along the way and that He delights in releasing His Kingdom in the world through us.

How can we be sure? Because we carry the Kingdom of heaven within us—an internal authority to pray God's Kingdom into the affairs of earth. We are praying from heaven to earth.

Jesus' internal authority set Him apart in His earthly ministry. People of the first century understood the external authority that accompanied the positions of the religious and civic leaders. Yet they could not understand the authority Jesus carried. Matthew 7:29 says that "He taught them as one having authority, and not as the scribes." This was not external but internal authority flowing from the secret place of life-giving prayer with His Father.

King David demonstrated a life of both external and internal authority. Anointed as king, he walked in external authority with grace and integrity that set him apart as a great king and warrior in Israel. But David also possessed internal authority. He knew God in the secret place through intimate life-giving worship and prayer. David carried the eternal Kingdom of God within him.

And so do you.

God's Gracious Design
"Your will be done on earth as it is in heaven."
MATTHEW 6:10

Do you ever add the phrase *If it be Your will* to your prayers? You probably mean to submit your requests to the will of God and the Lordship of Jesus Christ. But an incomplete understanding of this phrase—which is a very rich part of Jesus' model prayer—can end up causing us to settle for less than Jesus intended. It can also make this phrase a bit of a disclaimer, as if we don't know what God's will is and realize that if our prayer is not granted, it must not have been His will.

This is not what Jesus meant by the phrase *Your will be done*. When you pray out of that life-giving relationship in the secret place, your prayers are already aligned with the Father's will.

Will means determination, choice, purpose, decree, gracious design, inclination, desire, pleasure. It also means intend or intentions.

When we proclaim God's will on earth, we release the decrees of heaven into the affairs of earth. We are praying for God's purposes to unfold on earth. How rich it is to pray God's will from heaven to earth!

Things on earth, apart from God, get very chaotic. People not aligned with His Kingdom operate in chaos and lawlessness. The systems of the world—from families to businesses to governments—do not operate, apart from God, at their potential. Families struggle. Nations conflict with nations. World economies become dismantled.

Yet God has a design. He is not sitting in heaven wringing His hands and wondering what to do with this world He created. He has a will—an intentional design—for the affairs of this earth. God's will is His heavenly template, the gracious design of heaven's Kingdom that He wishes to manifest on earth. In our heavenly conversations in the secret place, God shows us this gracious design, so we can proclaim His will, His intentions, in the earth. We are, in a sense, laying the template of God's gracious design over the chaos on planet earth.

Will also means to delight in or to love something. Everything about heaven delights God. So when we proclaim His will on earth, we are embracing the delights of heaven and releasing heaven's atmosphere on earth.

Living from Heaven to Earth

If we are to *pray* from heaven to earth, we also need to *live* from heaven to earth. I think of living from heaven to earth this way: Heaven is my home and earth is where I live.

My job, for example, is my occupation, my vocation. I enjoy my work and find it very fulfilling, but I don't live there. At the end of the day, I leave my work behind to go home. My home is where I live, where I rest. I keep my belongings, my treasures, at home. My home is where my relationships flourish and where I am nourished. It is where I start and end the day.

But heaven is my real home.

The secret place I experience that heavenly climate where I meditate on the wonder of God while His words wash over me with life-giving force, transforming me into His gracious design. Heaven infuses everything I do with joy and creativity. I have heavenly conversation with God. I find rest and nurture as I abide in His presence. He is my shelter and safe refuge when life on earth seems really hard. This heavenly atmosphere is where I long to be.

When I dwell in the secret place with God, I can step out of the atmosphere of earth to partner with God to bring heaven to earth. How? I carry His Kingdom within me, so I can pray, "Your will be done on earth as it is in heaven."

Ephesians 2:2 tells us that Satan is "the prince of the power of the air." He does not live in heaven; he was cast down from heaven. Nor was earth created for him. So he does everything he can to turn mankind away from God's gracious design. Satan lives and operates in the atmosphere to try to displace a spiritual climate of faith with unbelief. He tries to supplant trust with fear, hope with despair, love with hate, and acceptance with rejection. He tries to undermine the goodness and light of God on earth.

Believers are atmosphere-transformers in the opposite way. The Kingdom of heaven within us gives us authority over the prince of the power of the air. Ephesians 2:6 says that we are seated with Christ in heavenly places. We are seated above that atmosphere where Satan engages in his dark tactics. We are seated with Christ to demonstrate the great grace of God that dispels darkness.

From that position with Christ, we can pray, "Your kingdom come. Your will be done on earth as it is in heaven." Our prayers can actually transform the atmosphere around us from unbelief to faith, from fear to trust, from despair to hope, from hate to love, from rejection to acceptance. An atmosphere that is life-draining becomes life-giving when we proclaim the will of God, His delight and gracious design, from heaven to earth.

Some time ago my husband, Dave, and I prayed to transform the spiritual atmosphere in part of a nearby community. We drove through the streets and prayed especially for the businesses. We felt drawn to a particular area of town in which we discovered an adult bookstore and video store in an otherwise family-oriented area. We could sense the darkness and oppressiveness that had come into that part of town. Yet we knew we were seated with Christ above the darkness, positioned to proclaim life and lay God's template over that community to bring His gracious design for the people living there.

So we prayed for the owners of that adult store. We prayed that God would release creativity in them for a new business plan that would be more profitable than their current pursuit. We prayed that they would prosper in a way that would bless the community and upgrade the neighborhood.

Sometime later, we noticed that the property had been sold, and we learned that the sale had been very profitable. The space ended up being used for developing educational pursuits in the community.

God had a design, His will, to bless and develop that community. Dave and I had been able to partner with heaven in prayer to overcome the prince of the power of the air and to reestablish heaven's influence over that part of town.

You, too, can live from heaven to earth, praying not with worry or negativity but with confidence, joy and a heart of worship. Praying from heaven to earth will help you and those around you to thrive rather than just survive. Praying from heaven to earth positions you to be an atmosphere-changer on earth.

8

Receiving the Resources of Heaven

"Give us this day our daily bread."
MATTHEW 6:11

Jesus did not worry about His daily needs. We are not to worry about ours either. He taught us that our Father knows our daily needs even before we ask.

Jesus was so free of concern about finding shelter at night that He actually made His bed in a rocking boat as it was tossed on a stormy sea (see Mark 4:37–38). How could He rest so serenely in the middle of a life-threatening storm? Because in the secret place with His Father, Jesus had learned to reach beyond the resources of earth to receive the resources of heaven.

He needed shelter and rest that night, and the resources of earth offered only the stern of a fishing boat on a stormy sea. But Jesus reached into the resources of heaven to find the inner peace and comfort that would transform a storm-tossed boat into a place of serenity. Then, when those around Him were overcome with fear, He reached into the resources of heaven to transform the atmosphere and calm the storm.

Jesus did not worry about finances either. He did not panic when the Temple tax was due. Instead of trying to figure out how to exempt Himself from paying the tax, Jesus reached beyond the resources of earth and into the resources of heaven. The resources of earth that day were Peter's fishing skills. The resources of heaven: a coin miraculously found in the fish's mouth—just enough to pay their taxes (see Matthew 17:24–27).

Another day they needed food—a lot of food. Everyone was hungry after a big day of teaching and ministry. When Jesus' disciples checked their earthly resources, they became really stressed. They did not have nearly enough to feed more than five thousand people. The only resource earth offered that day was a little boy's lunch, so the disciples wanted to send everyone home to take care of themselves.

What did Jesus do? He did not deliver a sermon on world hunger or fasting. He did not even receive an offering. Instead He reached beyond the resources of earth, and heaven supplied enough to feed the whole crowd, plus a take-home container for each disciple.

When Jesus needed something, He did not ignore the resources of earth; yet He was not limited by earth's resources either. He used what earth had to offer to reach for something higher—something limitless, something earth could not provide. He could do this because of His confident relationship with His Father in the secret place.

Daily Bread

When Jesus instructed His disciples to pray in the secret place for "daily bread," He referred to their need for temporal sustenance—food, clothing, the daily necessities of life. *Daily bread* also refers to the spiritual substance that gives us life. The power of prayer in the secret place is the result of abiding continually in God's presence and feeding on the life-giving substance of who He is.

David understood how to draw daily on the substance of God's presence. He wrote, "The Lord is my shepherd; I shall not want" (Psalm 23:1). In other words, we will be in need of nothing.

When a small boy was memorizing the 23rd Psalm, he was taught to repeat only two or three words at a time. So he repeated the words over and over until he finally memorized the first phrase: "The Lord is my shepherd." His teacher, thinking that one phrase was sufficient for the child to memorize, said, "That's enough." The boy repeated, "That's enough." Afterward, whenever he quoted Psalm 23:1, he said, "The Lord is my shepherd and that's enough."

His misquote was an excellent and insightful paraphrase. As we know the loving care of the Lord, we have everything we need. He is enough.

We can gain another insight into the "daily bread" of the Lord's Prayer by looking at Psalm 23: "You prepare a table before me in the presence of my enemies" (verse 5a). This refers to the code of conduct governing the king's camp on the battlefield. When his table was set in that dangerous place, the seating area became a safety zone, like an embassy—off limits to the enemy.

The table the Lord prepares for us is safe in the same way. In the middle of hardship and battle, our Lord has prepared His table for us. The chaos raging around us is not allowed near the King's table. When we draw near to Him, our strength is renewed and life is restored. He welcomes us daily to meet with Him. He Himself is our daily bread.

Our Treasure And Our Heart

God is a giver. He delights in blessing us and satisfying all our needs. But He also wants us to know the joy and fulfillment of giving. When we give into His Kingdom or give to bless others, we express His loving and giving nature. Giving is one way we grow to be more like Him.

Just a few verses after teaching His disciples the Lord's Prayer, Jesus told them,

> "Do not lay up for yourselves treasures on earth, where moth and rust destroy and where thieves break in and steal; but lay up for yourselves treasures in heaven, where neither moth nor rust destroys and where thieves do not break in and steal. For where your treasure is, there your heart will be also."
>
> MATTHEW 6:19–21

Giving draws us deeper into the rich relationship with God in the secret place. The Message translation puts it this way: "The place where your treasure is, is the place you will most want to be, and end up being" (verse 21).

Dave and I have explored the blessing of giving. We have found that giving is one key to receiving from the Lord. And giving opens the door to a deep place in God's treasury that goes beyond having our needs met. God takes us to a dimension of relationship with Him that releases His wisdom and creativity into our stewardship. When we give generously of the resources He has given us, He shows us how to access our "treasures in heaven" (Matthew 6:20)—those gifts we have deposited there. The Lord shows us the limitlessness of heaven's resources.

9

The Liberty of Forgiveness

"And forgive us our debts, as we forgive our debtors."
MATTHEW 6:12

Offenses can lodge in our soul. When we are offended, we can experience a nagging ache that leads to anger, depression or a preoccupation for revenge. Not forgiving an offense can paralyze us emotionally from the freedom and abundant life that Jesus offers us. Likewise, when we have offended others, the guilt we carry can separate us from trusting relationships and lead us to difficulty in forgiving ourselves.

Forgiveness, on the other hand, brings liberty. When we forgive others their offenses, they are liberated from the guilt of their actions or the pain they have caused. Furthermore, we are liberated from the pain we have carried from those offenses. And when God forgives us of the sins of our past, we are set free from the power that sin holds on our future. When we forgive, we are free to receive forgiveness.

The Miracle of Forgiveness

That God could forgive our sins and give us eternal life is unquestionably a miracle. It is also a miracle for us to forgive one another. It takes God's grace flowing through us.

There is a deep place in our heart that holds the capacity for forgiveness or unforgiveness. Hebrews 12:14–15 admonishes us to keep that place cleansed by the grace of God:

> Pursue peace with all people, and holiness, without which no one will see the Lord: looking carefully lest anyone fall short of the grace of God; lest any root of bitterness springing up cause trouble, and by this many become defiled.

In other words, we are to keep ourselves clear of offending others or being offended by others, either one of which hinders our relationships.

The English poet Alexander Pope (1688–1744) wrote, "To err is human; to forgive, divine." While he intended that line in "An Essay on Criticism" to be a satirical comment, it is actually a true and powerful statement. We need God's nature imparted to us if we are to forgive. We receive this intimate impartation through life-giving prayer as God enables us to forgive. As we know His kindness, goodness, grace, patience and forgiveness deeply, we are free to forgive others deeply.

And as we hear Jesus pray, "Father, forgive them" (Luke 23:34), there is an awakening of His grace within us that releases the miracle of forgiveness in our hearts. When we pray for those who have hurt us, grace and forgiveness flow through us.

We must forgive in order to be forgiven. Jesus explained,

"For if you forgive men their trespasses, your heavenly Father will also forgive you. But if you do not forgive men their trespasses, neither will your Father forgive your trespasses."

MATTHEW 6:14–15

Forgiveness is non-negotiable. We find the miracle of God's grace to forgive and the power to overcome offense in God's loving embrace in the secret place.

The Reward of Forgiveness

To know God truly is to know forgiveness. Knowing the grace of being forgiven is foundational to our relationship with Him. Then, as we forgive others, His grace is perfected in us.

Years ago Dave and I were hurt in a situation that seemed unfounded and unfair. We felt that any impartial observer, if we took the opportunity to defend ourselves, would clearly see how unfairly we had been treated. Yet as we prayed about the situation, we sensed the Holy Spirit saying, *When you start defending yourselves, that's when I'll stop defending you.* It did not matter how right we were. What mattered was the condition of our hearts. We knew then that we needed to sacrifice self-defense and embrace the life-giving flow of forgiveness.

And as we forgave, our hearts were healed of the hurt we had experienced. We saw numerous ways God brought growth into our lives and into the lives of others as forgiveness freed us all from that offense.

The apostle Stephen had an encounter with God that empowered him to forgive (see Acts 7:55–60). After a revelation of heaven, he was able to forgive his accusers as they stoned him. Stephen's prayer sounds similar to Jesus' words when

He forgave the thief crucified next to Him. Stephen said as he was being stoned to death, "Lord, do not charge them with this sin" (verse 60). Even as he was being martyred, Stephen's heart flowed with the power and grace of God.

Such grace opened the door for the early Church to spread throughout Judea and Samaria. Many came to life in Christ when one man forgave.

One of the sons of the patriarch Jacob also learned the grace to forgive. Throughout his life Joseph had many opportunities to hold a grudge. His brothers kidnapped him, beat him and sold him into slavery. Then, as a slave working for the Egyptian official Potiphar, Joseph was accused falsely by Potiphar's wife and imprisoned. Later his fellow prisoner, the chief butler, forgot about him after his own release, though Joseph had interpreted his dream and asked him to put in a good word with Pharaoh.

Joseph, a man of dreams and talents, was abused and neglected in many ways. He had every right to be bitter, hurt and angry.

In Genesis 42, after Joseph was vindicated and placed in command over all the resources of the land of Egypt, his brothers who had abused and betrayed him came to him seeking to buy grain during the famine. This could have been Joseph's opportunity for revenge. Yet he forgave them. Where did he find such grace?

Something happened in Joseph between the time the butler was released from prison and when Joseph was summoned to serve in Pharaoh's court. Genesis 41:1 indicates this was a period of two years. It was a silent period in the narrative of the Bible. All we know about Joseph during this time is that he continued to serve in prison under false charges. It was a time of hiddenness in Joseph's life. Joseph was in the secret place with God receiving a deep, intimate impartation of grace to forgive.

Joseph expressed the depth of his forgiveness toward his brothers when he said,

> "You meant evil against me; but God meant it for good, in order to bring it about as it is this day, to save many people alive. Now therefore, do not be afraid; I will provide for you and your little ones." And he comforted them and spoke kindly to them.
>
> GENESIS 50:20–21

Out of the depth of Joseph's experience with God, he forgave and blessed them. Hope and life were restored to his brothers and their families, and they were given food and invited to live in a place of plenty during a time of famine. When Joseph forgave, he was restored to relationship with his family.

Job, too, knew God in the secret place. We read in Job 19 about the agony of his losses and the pain he endured. Yet in the middle of his discourse on the severity of his suffering, he raised his voice in worship and declared,

> "I know that my Redeemer lives, and He shall stand at last on the earth; and after my skin is destroyed, this I know, that in my flesh I shall see God, whom I shall see for myself, and my eyes shall behold, and not another. How my heart yearns within me!"
>
> JOB 19:25–27

Job did not use his suffering as an excuse to turn from God. Instead, his suffering drove him deeper into the treasury of God in the secret place.

The only good thing about Job's friends—who were not very good friends—is that they visited him frequently. But instead of offering encouragement, comfort or help, they added to his torment with endless questions, accusations and judgments against him. Finally, near the end of Job's story, God confronted those friends. He told them that He was angry with them and that they needed to ask Job to pray for them. Only then, perhaps, would He receive their sacrifices and forgive them (see Job 42:7–9).

Once again a godly man faced the need to forgive. Something had to happen in Job's heart to enable him to pray sincerely for his friends. He had to forgive them, too.

Job's losses were restored through the grace of forgiveness:

> The Lord restored Job's losses *when he prayed for his friends*. Indeed the Lord gave Job twice as much as he had before.
>
> JOB 42:10 (ITALICS ADDED)

Palal Intercession

The word translated "pray" in Job 42 is *palal*. It refers to asking someone with more power and wisdom to intervene on behalf of the one praying. *Palal* comes from the root word that means "to judge." *Palal* is intercession to the One with the power and authority to clear the record of all wrongdoing and forgive every offense and sin.

For Job, *palal* intercession released forgiveness, which God alone had the power and wisdom to grant. Job prayed and God forgave. *Palal* intercession often releases the power of God's forgiveness.

Palal intercession occurs numerous times throughout the Old Testament. Jonah's place of *palal* intercession, his secret place of prayer, was the belly of a large fish. His *palal* intercession brought forgiveness to him for his disobedience. Jonah, in turn, brought a message of repentance and forgiveness to the whole region of Nineveh.

Moses made *palal* intercession on behalf of the people of Israel. God's anger against them ceased and His forgiveness was released. Because Moses walked with God and knew Him in the secret place, he could intervene on behalf of the people, asking God on their behalf for forgiveness.

Palal intercession appears in this very familiar Scripture on prayer—the one I thought of when Dave and I were praying with the students for his school:

> "If My people who are called by My name will humble themselves, and pray and seek My face, and turn from their wicked ways, then I will hear from heaven, and will forgive their sin and heal their land."
>
> 2 CHRONICLES 7:14

We often quote this Scripture for special prayer days or events such as the National Day of Prayer. The power of this prayer to heal the land lies in the One who has the power to forgive. The sins of our nation are forgiven not just because many people pray. Righteous values are not restored due to a large prayer event or commitment to an extended fast. Our nation is forgiven and healed solely because of *palal* intercession. It is because we appeal to the One with the wisdom and power to intervene. We are forgiven because we intercede with the One who has the power and authority to clear the record of any judgment against us.

When this verse says, "If My people . . . will humble themselves," humbling refers to a lifestyle of bowing before God. It is an ongoing relationship of worship in the secret place, acknowledging the greatness of God and His power and authority to forgive.

When we forgive, He will forgive.

10

Overcoming Evil

"And do not lead us into temptation, but deliver us from the evil one."

MATTHEW 6:13

We all deal with hardship, temptation and spiritual warfare. These issues can become very draining. A constant battle with temptation, especially when we resist, can wear us down. Facing the schemes of the wicked one can be exhausting even when we rise above his harassment.

The Perspective of the Secret Place

In the life-giving prayer relationship of the secret place, spiritual warfare takes on a perspective of victory and triumph. In the secret place, we are truly delivered from evil. In God's presence, which is full of the light of His glory and majesty, we are free.

We hear a lot of teaching on spiritual warfare that emphasizes knowing the enemy and understanding the devices the wicked one uses against us. Such knowledge can be helpful. But too much emphasis on knowing the wicked one can also be detrimental. It can cause us to be overly impressed with him and fascinated with evil. This is oppressive and defeating.

In the secret place of worship and prayer, we meditate on the goodness, greatness and power of God. Our pursuit is to know God in His vastness and majesty. In that place, there is no room for any preoccupation with the power of the evil one. As we are overwhelmed with God's goodness, we are absolutely unimpressed with evil. This is the perspective of the secret place on spiritual warfare.

We are not naïve. Satan possesses dark power. He has wreaked havoc in our lives and in the world. Yet in comparison to the goodness and kindness of God, Satan's schemes are fleeting. When contrasted with to the glorious riches of Christ, the thief who steals, kills and destroys is just a nuisance. In comparison to the manifold wisdom and majesty of God, the wicked one is unimpressive.

The Safety of the Secret Place

The secret place of worship and prayer is a place of refuge and safety and security. Consider these psalms:

> You shall hide them in the secret place of Your presence from the plots of man; You shall keep them secretly in a pavilion from the strife of tongues.
>
> PSALM 31:20

> He who dwells in the secret place of the Most High shall abide under the shadow of the Almighty. I will say of the Lord, "He is my refuge and my fortress; my God, in Him I will trust." Surely He shall deliver you from the snare of the fowler and from the perilous pestilence.
>
> PSALM 91:1–3

You are my hiding place; You shall preserve me
from trouble; You shall surround me with songs
of deliverance. Selah.

PSALM 32:7

In God's presence no evil thing can harm or oppress us, and
no power of darkness can overtake us.

Victory in the Secret Place

God promises a way of escape from temptation:

No temptation has overtaken you except such as is
common to man; but God is faithful, who will not
allow you to be tempted beyond what you are able,
but with the temptation will also make the way of
escape, that you may be able to bear it.

1 CORINTHIANS 10:13

Where is that way of escape? In the secret place. When we are
closeted alone with God in worship and prayer, the wicked
one simply cannot invade. The secret place, then, is our escape hatch. The powers of darkness may rush at us with all
manner of evil, but we become invisible to the wicked one
when we slip into that secret place with our Father. This is
confounding to the evil one and victory for us.

When we understand the anatomy of temptation, we see
how our deliverance comes in the secret place. We are tempted in body and soul (consisting of mind, will and emotions).
When you enter the secret place in your spirit, your body and
soul will follow into the refuge of God. In the secret place,
your spirit is transformed and renewed. Your spirit is filled

with the power of the Holy Spirit. You receive divine wisdom to know how to deal with the evil that confronts you. Through your spirit, your mind receives divine strategies to flee temptation. With the manifold wisdom of God and the authority of Christ in you, you can triumph over any temptation. Your spirit empowers your emotions to receive the grace, peace and joy you need to be an overcomer. Your spirit rises up full of God's glory and wrapped in His majesty. With the strength of an overcomer, you can be victorious over the destructive schemes that come against you.

Your flesh may be tempted with immorality, addiction, violence, murder or any other such act of sin. Perhaps your mind is drawn into deception or oppressive thoughts. Those thoughts lead to all sorts of life-draining emotions—hate, self-pity, discouragement, anger, hopelessness. You can find deliverance from those temptations in the secret place.

So whenever you face temptation, run into the safety of the loving presence of God. There your heart will be lifted in worship of your Father. You will be encouraged as you listen to Jesus pray for you with tenderness and authority. And the Holy Spirit will show you His strategy to draw you to a greater life of triumph. Instead of struggling to pray against the temptation, begging for victory or sinking into a pit of oppressive thoughts and emotions, you will find peace and life in God's presence. The temptation will turn to victory as your heart swells with praise of His goodness and majesty.

Satan may be crafty and wily and imitative, but he is not creative. In the secret place, God shows you the predictable patterns the wicked one uses to try to lead you into temptation. The secret place is teeming with creativity. Isn't that what you would expect in the presence of the Creator? God will give you creative insights to change the atmosphere around you and overcome the dark oppressiveness of the tempter.

Jesus taught us to pray, "Do not lead us into temptation." He gives you creative new paths that lead away from those old patterns of the wicked one. The Holy Spirit will show you new paths, new ways of doing things that lead to righteousness, joy and peace.

You may find that you struggle with temptation because of the atmosphere at home or at work or in your community. You may be surrounded by people who are disparaging or harassing and weigh on your emotions. But in the secret place, you will receive creative thoughts and divine insight to know how to rise up and change the atmosphere. You will be transformed from a person swayed by the atmosphere to a person who sways the atmosphere. You overcome an atmosphere of defeat with the atmosphere of the secret place within you.

The Battle Belongs to the Lord

In a message on the secret place, Graham Cooke said,

> You don't have to fight the enemy over everything. Sometimes you just need to know how to step back into the secret place and just wait. There are times when the enemy wants you to fight him. You only fight him when God tells you to fight him. There are times when you have to step back into your refuge, and you let God defend you. You ignore the enemy. You don't have to go attack or contest things with the enemy every time—you only do it when God tells you to do it. The rest of the time you are to be occupied with Jesus.

In 2 Chronicles 20 King Jehoshaphat and his people met with God in prayer—in the secret place—for a battle plan. The Lord said, "The battle is not yours, but God's. . . . Position yourselves, stand still and see the salvation of the Lord" (verses 15, 17). God was saying, "Ignore the enemy. Stay hidden in Me and watch Me deliver you."

Instead of sending soldiers into battle, then, Jehoshaphat called for the biggest worship service they could muster. And God defeated the enemy armies. Jehoshaphat and his people went out to survey the spoils of battle and found an overflowing abundance of treasure. It was more than they could carry, and it took three days to gather it all. They were so blessed that they named the area the Valley of Berachah, which means "Valley of Blessing."

How did Jehoshaphat's valley of battle become the Valley of Blessing? Instead of rushing out to fight his own battle, which looked hopeless, he inquired of the Lord in the secret place. God said not to fight, so he did not fight; he worshiped. He stayed hidden in God, and God was Israel's defender. The king gathered the treasure and celebrated the blessing of God.

When the wicked one taunts you to draw you into battle, draw deeper into the secret place and inquire of the Lord. If God does not say go out and fight, then stay hidden in Him and worship. Let Him be your defender and victor, and watch God turn your valley of battle to the abundance of His blessing.

Sometimes when we inquire of the Lord, He gives us a battle plan. When we engage in battle, we do so at the direct command of the Captain of the host, Jesus—in agreement with Him, by the power of the Holy Spirit and under the protection of our Father. He "always leads us in triumph" (2 Corinthians 2:14) because He has already conquered every scheme of the wicked one.

At that point, we engage in the spiritual battle proactively. We are on the offense rather than the defense. In sports terms, we have the ball and are ready to score, rather than trying to prevent the adversary from scoring against us.

A point of clarification: For God to *lead* us in triumph, we have to *follow* Him. Sometimes following Him means going deeper into the hiddenness of the secret place. At other times it means engaging in the battle so full of the Holy Spirit, and clothed in the authority of Christ, that the very scent of victory on us causes the wicked one to flee (see 2 Corinthians 2:14–16). Either way, we know the battle is the Lord's and that He will lead us to victory.

The Secret Place and the Battleground

The Father and the Holy Spirit sealed the baptism of Jesus by making their presence evident. Then, after His baptism, Jesus was led by the Holy Spirit into the wilderness, where He stayed for forty days. The wilderness was a place of solitude where Jesus was set apart from distractions. He was also fasting. What goes along with fasting? Prayer.

Jesus' time in the wilderness was not for solitary confinement. He went there to spend time with His Father as He prepared to launch His earthly ministry. The wilderness was a secret place of prayer.

Between the times of prayer and listening to His Father, the tempter came. But Jesus had the strength He needed to face temptation on that battleground because He was with His Father there. The Son of God was full of the Holy Spirit and had a ready answer to defeat the tempter because He had already heard from His Father. Before the wilderness became a spiritual battleground, Jesus had made it His secret place.

Jesus followed this pattern throughout His life. We already noted that in Mark 4, when the disciples were terrified in a life-threatening storm on the sea, Jesus slept peacefully in the stern of the boat. While His disciples gave in to the temptation to fear, Jesus made His secret place in the midst of turmoil. The secret place with His Father was established within Him. The storm was not a battleground to Him. It was a place of inner peace because He carried the peace of the Father within Him.

Jesus' greatest spiritual battle took place in Gethsemane shortly before His crucifixion. Yet Jesus had met with His Father there, too, as He went to that garden frequently to pray. While He battled His own will and agonized as He faced the suffering of the cross, Jesus was victorious because He already had history with His Father there. Before it was ever a battleground, it was a secret place.

If there is an area where you are vulnerable to temptation or spiritual battle, build a sanctuary there. Intentionally fellowship with God and embrace His presence. You will be so full of the strength of the Holy Spirit and the wisdom of God that you will have a ready answer when the tempter comes. You will already have the history with God to make that a place of victory and life in His presence.

My husband, Dave, practices this on his job. Criticism, selfish hidden agendas and secret sin used to darken the atmosphere of his workplace. But after battling the frustration and temptation to respond in ways he did not like, Dave began to make his workplace a prayer sanctuary. As he lived in an awareness of God's presence, the wicked one no longer harassed him in the same ways. The atmosphere at work actually changed from frustration to blessing. The former battleground became fertile for God's goodness.

Spiritual Warfare from the Secret Place

We find the key to spiritual warfare in a classic passage of Scripture:

> We do not wrestle against flesh and blood, but against principalities, against powers, against the

> rulers of the darkness of this age, against spiritual hosts of wickedness in the heavenly places. Therefore take up the whole armor of God, that you may be able to withstand in the evil day, and having done all, to stand . . . praying always with all prayer and supplication in the Spirit, being watchful to this end with all perseverance and supplication for all the saints.
>
> EPHESIANS 6:12–13, 18

This passage explains both spiritual warfare and the hierarchy of dark spirits. It also shows us the powerful and effective spiritual armor we have in Christ. Yet the key, as we see in verse 18, is prayer: "Praying always with all prayer and supplication."

"Prayer" here refers to all manner of prayer—thanksgiving, asking, requesting. "Supplication" means to seek earnestly for benefits. When we ask for God's benefits, we are not begging God to meet our most meager needs; we are seeking His blessing and favor. In this way, in the middle of spiritual warfare, we can flourish and thrive rather than merely survive.

In spiritual warfare we need to seek the benefits, blessings and rewards God has for us. Well-meaning believers can become discouraged, even oppressed, when they are caught up in the battle. They can become so preoccupied with raising the sword that they overlook God's blessing and neglect to raise their voices in worship. When we focus on the powers of darkness, we can miss the revelation of God's majesty.

Daniel 10 gives an account of spiritual warfare. In a heavenly conversation, Daniel gained insight about a spiritual battle. He saw how the Holy Spirit was working on earth and in the atmosphere. God also showed him the future. But Daniel wrote, "When he spoke to me I was strengthened" (verse 19). In that secret place the man of God was encouraged rather than spiritually drained.

If we have lost our joy or peace, then we have lost a battle. When spiritual warfare becomes life-draining, it is time to go deeper into the secret place for that life-giving prayer relationship with God to be restored. There our inner joy, peace and strength will be renewed and refreshed. When we live in the deep presence of God, our soul prospers through every battle. In the secret place we obtain the spiritual insight to gain advantage in the battle.

Proclamation That Overcomes Evil

We see one final insight to overcoming evil in Revelation 12:11: "They overcame him by the blood of the Lamb and by the word of their testimony, and they did not love their lives to the death."

A "testimony" is the declaration of a witness speaking with the authority of one who knows. It is a prevailing proclamation. Our proclamation is empowered and full of life out of the time we spend in the secret place of prayer. When we receive a word from the Lord there, we receive God's proclamation filled with the power and wisdom of heaven. That proclamation carries the authenticity of the One we relate with intimately through prayer.

The word of our testimony is not what we know; it is who we know. At the word of such a proclamation, hell trembles and we overcome the wicked one.

I mentioned earlier that my husband has made his workplace a sanctuary of prayer. Dave knows by experience that God brings order and an environment for young people to be educated and nurtured toward their destinies. With that testimony, he has learned to proclaim God's peace and blessing whenever something causes chaos on the campus. A simple yet powerful proclamation of God's goodness resets the atmosphere.

There are times when I begin to become frustrated, discouraged or weary with the circumstances around me. Often in the secret place of prayer, I hear the Lord say, *My grace is sufficient.* I have *more than enough grace for both of us.* That becomes my proclamation that breaks through anxiety and restores me to peace: God's grace is more than enough!

In John 16:33 Jesus said, "These things I have spoken to you, that in Me you may have peace. In the world you will have tribulation; but be of good cheer, I have overcome the world." If you want peace, abide with the Prince of Peace. If you want to be an overcomer, abide with the One who has overcome the world.

11

Fruitful Life, Fruitful Prayer

For Yours is the kingdom and the power and the
glory forever. Amen.

MATTHEW 6:13

Fruitfulness is in the nature of God. He intends for us to be
fruitful, too. When we dwell with Him in the secret place,
our lives become fruitful. And the prayer that results from
that deep relationship is relevant and rewarding.

Jesus never intended for our lives to be stagnant or our
prayers meaningless. He has much to say about the fruitfulness that overflows from our lives as we live in Him: "He who
abides in Me, and I in him, bears much fruit" (John 15:5). Not
only that, but Jesus intends that His life through us will bear
fruit in exponential proportions: "He who believes in Me,
the works that I do he will do also; and greater works than
these he will do, because I go to My Father" (John 14:12). He
also promised we would have "whatever you ask in My name"
(John 14:13) and that we can expect His abundance to flow
through our lives (see John 10:10).

What do we need in order for these things to happen?

As we saw in chapter 4, "faith as a mustard seed" (Matthew 17:20)—something small with the capacity to grow into something big. The prayer of faith has the capacity for great results. Our prayer is like a seed that seems small and lifeless when isolated. Yet just as the seed that springs to life and explodes into fruitfulness when planted in the soil, so our prayer overflows with life when we are hidden in deep communion with God. We are transformed into carriers of light and life as we dwell in the presence of the Giver of light and life.

We have seen that as we pray and worship in the secret place, we see things differently. We see from heaven's view with a depth of revelation of God and His ways. Our minds are renewed to think with the limitlessness of heaven, no longer bound by the confines of the world's mindset. As we see differently, we pray fruitfully because we are praying *with* God rather than just *to* Him.

Fruitful prayer fully relates with God: knowing Him, listening, observing, conversing with Him and proclaiming His intent. As we pray in the secret place of God's habitation, He unfolds His ways, His wisdom and His power to us to bear fruit from our praying.

In deep communion with God, we understand how to access the promises and resources of heaven to release the fullness of His blessing in our lives. Our way of life is described in Ephesians 3:19–20, where Paul prayed that his readers would

> know the love of Christ which passes knowledge; that you may be filled with all the fullness of God. Now to Him who is able to do exceedingly abundantly above all that we ask or think, according to the power that works in us, to Him be glory in the church by Christ Jesus to all generations, forever and ever. Amen.

What is the secret? You know it already:

> "But you, when you pray, go into your room, and
> when you have shut your door, pray to your Father
> who is in the secret place; and your Father who sees
> in secret will reward you openly."
>
> MATTHEW 6:6

Heaven's Open Door

Prayer opens the door to all the provision, abundant life and revelation that our Father has for us. Our Lord is eager to speak to us and to bless us. He has invited us into His presence where He can show us the majesty of His Kingdom. John saw this in a vision:

> After these things I looked, and behold, a door
> standing open in heaven. And the first voice which
> I heard was like a trumpet speaking with me, say-
> ing, "Come up here, and I will show you things
> which must take place after this."
>
> REVELATION 4:1

God draws us into that heavenly realm where we view the affairs of earth from His perspective. He shows us the richness of His power, grace and resources to go beyond just meeting our needs. As we see from His heavenly realm, He shows us how the issues on earth are working together to bring the fullness of His Kingdom into our lives so we flourish spiritually. When we pray, heaven's door opens so we can see beyond our earthly experiences and embrace eternal life.

As we are transported into this heavenly realm through prayer, we enter a depth of worship that comes from seeing the majesty of God. Our prayer becomes less about us and more about Him.

For Yours is the Kingdom, O God. You are the majestic One, the sovereign One. Let all the kingdoms of this earth know that You alone are God. Let the intentions of Your heart be demonstrated in the earth.

For Yours is the power, O God. You alone have the power to redeem us. You alone have the power to bring the chaos of earth into the order of heaven. Display Your power in us and through us.

Show us Your glory, O God. We are drawn toward Your goodness and glory. The light of Your presence gives us joy and hope. When we see Your glory, we, too, arise as an expression of the light of Your glory.

Your kingdom, Your power and Your glory give us life.

> For Yours is the kingdom and the power and the glory forever. Amen.
>
> Matthew 6:13

CPSIA information can be obtained at www.ICGtesting.com
Printed in the USA
LVOW13s0158110913

351676LV00001B/5/P